OUTDOOR SPACES

OUTDOOR SPACES

LANDSCAPE DESIGN FOR TODAY'S LIVING

JACK MAGUIRE

PRINCIPAL PHOTOGRAPHER
DEREK FELL

HENRY HOLT AND COMPANY
NEW YORK

A Quarto Book

Copyright © 1987 by Quarto Marketing Ltd.

Published by Henry Holt and Company, Inc.,
521 Fifth Avenue, New York, N.Y. 10175.

Library of Congress Cataloging-in-Publication Data

Maguire, Jack.
Outdoor spaces

Includes index.
1. Garden structures—Design and construction.
2. Landscape architecture. I. Title.
TH4961.M39 1987   712'.6   86-18358
ISBN 0-8050-0057-7

OUTDOOR SPACES
Landscape Design for Today's Living
was prepared and produced by
Quarto Marketing Ltd.
15 West 26th Street
New York, N.Y. 10010

Editor: Pamela Hoenig
Art Director: Mary Moriarty
Designer: Robert W. Kosturko
Photo Editor/Photo Researcher: Susan M. Duane
Production Manager: Karen L. Greenberg

First Edition

Typeset by I, CLAVDIA
Phototypesetting & Graphic Design Inc.
Color separations by South Seas Graphic Art Co.
Printed and bound in Hong Kong by Leefung-Asco Printers Ltd.

1 3 5 7 9 10 8 6 4 2

ISBN 0-8050-0057-7

DEDICATION

To my brother, Paul Beck Maguire

ACKNOWLEDGMENTS

I'd like to thank
Jill Myers and James H. Roper
for their expert recommendations.

CONTENTS

CONTENTS

PART ONE:

BEGINNING THE PROCESS

CHAPTER ONE

PLANNING YOUR OUTDOORS

Everyone knows that the great outdoors is meant for fun—especially that precious part of it that surrounds one's home. Yet, it's no surprise that many people do little to develop their property, leaving that task mainly to chance and nature. They feed and trim their lawn. They plant flowers around the foundation of their house. When the weather is nice, they set up a portable grill, a table and chairs and have a picnic. It's so pleasant simply to be out in the fresh air, gazing on a natural landscape, that they lull themselves into a state of complacency.

Unfortunately, their backyard isn't convenient for much besides passive enjoyment when the weather is fair. Meanwhile, they are confined to the house for most of their eating, socializing, playing, and lounging because the house has been carefully equipped for these functions. Soon boredom sets in and complacency begins to wane as they look beyond their windows to all that space just waiting to be inhabited.

In recent years, people have actively responded to major social, institutional, and technological changes by creating lifestyles to fit their own specialized needs and talents. As a result, people have become much more concerned and knowledgeable about home design. They look for living arrangements that are practical, flexible, and distinctive and that utilize the full potential of the home environment. When striving for these objectives, there are no separate standards for outdoor and indoor spaces. Both areas demand the same high degree of creativity and care. Both need to accommodate various functional as well as aesthetic considerations if they are to contribute to the quality of daily life.

For entertaining or just relaxing , nothing beats a row of rocking chairs.

A playhouse can be fun and a beautiful addition to your landscape.

Outdoor Spaces will help you achieve both functional and aesthetic goals in the development of your property. This book outlines practical plans that not only reflect sound principles of style and efficiency but also incorporate personal and creative fantasies. *Outdoor Spaces* offers a wide range of specific ideas and examples, in text and illustrations, that are adaptable to individual domestic situations. Also included is a list of resources that you can tap to implement an overall outdoor design.

In this book you'll find four chapters defining and illustrating the four main functions that domestic outdoor areas are commonly asked to serve:

- **Entertaining**: lawns; decks; patios; shade and shelter structures; outdoor furniture; and facilities for eating and drinking;

- **Space for children**: playgrounds; play equipment; playhouses; tree houses; and sand, water, and plant environments;

- **Recreation**: swimming pools; hot tubs and spas; tennis courts; and multipurpose sport, exercise, and game areas;

- **Gardens**: flower gardens; herb and vegetable gardens; novelty gardens; water gardens; special plantings; greenhouses; fences; walls; walkways; and fountains.

A final chapter, "Practical and Decorative Accents," focuses on finishing touches you can use to accent your outdoor spaces to give them a more personal look.

KEY ELEMENTS OF OUTDOOR DESIGN

Your home is your land as well as your house, but there's no denying that the house takes preeminence in terms of conveying individual taste and lifestyle. The most effective plan for outdoor spaces, therefore, is one that works from the inside out—that carries over and restates the design intentions and functional capacities of the indoor spaces. This integration of the house with its surrounding property will give your total home environment a sense of unity—an essential factor in any successful design.

Striving for unity in planning your outdoor spaces does not necessarily mean that the colors, shapes, textures, and patterns you create for outdoor structures and land areas have to mirror these elements inside your home. Instead, it means that the general style, tone, and mood of your outdoor and indoor spaces should harmonize and create an appealing interplay of design styles.

A successful recreation area offers pleasure to the body and mind alike.

Planning a garden involves foresight, practicality, and the eye of an artist.

Above: *This white lath trellis-and-gate structure effectively restates the lines and materials of the clapboard house behind it.* Right: *A rainbow palette of small flowers adorning the top of a roughly constructed stone wall accents a wild garden.*

Sometimes this harmony is achieved by duplication; for example, by fashioning an elaborate ornamental garden as an extension of a baroque-style house filled with exquisitely detailed antiques. Other times a personal and effective style is achieved by contrast; for example, by cultivating a rustic country garden with meandering stone walls and walkways to complement a starkly furnished house of glass and steel. Either strategy involves the outdoors "speaking to" the indoors.

Unity also implies tying together the functional aspects of the indoors and the outdoors. Traffic needs to be able to flow smoothly and logically from the house to the yard, whether the people in your family are entertaining, gardening, playing, or doing all three activities at the same time. The view from the house's windows should be as attractive as the view outside the house. Decks, patios, and shade shelters should be designed and situated so that they work well in conjunction with their indoor counterparts.

In addition to unity, there are two other basic design considerations: balance and accent. Aiming toward balance in your outdoor plan is a matter of creating a rough equilibrium in scale and proportion among the various masses on your property. If your house dominates one corner of your property, for instance, you may want to locate a large outbuilding or a substantial grove of trees on the op-

posite corner of your property. If you have a low wall surrounding your patio, you may want to create some vertical point of interest in a nearby garden, such as a clump of tall specimen plants or a partial border of shrubs.

An accent is any object—or treatment of an object—that serves as a particularly striking focal point in your overall design. It may be a small statue in the center of a garden, or fanciful scrollwork around the roof of a gazebo, or a bold graphic imposed on the surface of a patio wall. Accents can attract the eye to outstanding features in the landscape, help to avoid monotony in a part of the yard that is relatively bland, or highlight a recurring theme in your design scheme. Too many accents, however, can produce a jarring effect. The trick is to be highly selective and choose those few accents that will have the most desirable impact.

MAKING PLANS

The best ideas for making your outdoor spaces both functional and attractive are those that come after you begin the formal process of planning. It's not a difficult process. In fact, it's a lot of fun—and it's a unique way of gaining insights not only about your home but also about yourself and your family.

At first glance this dramatic backyard space looks deceptively casual. Actually, it is a meticulously balanced arrangement of reflecting pools, trees, shrubs, and rectangular shapes.

15

The first step is to sketch a plan of your property as it exists now. Use graph paper (or paper you have lined yourself) and draw all the features of your yard to scale, including the space that your house and any other buildings occupy. Include entrances and exits to both the property and the house, window views, paths, trees, gardens, and such natural features as changes in grade, marshy areas, and rock outcroppings. Note all aboveground and underground utility lines and any easements that pose limitations on construction (for example, in many areas no permanent structure like a shed or deck can be closer than ten feet to public property, such as the street). Also mark the areas of shade and sun interplay at different times of the year and the prevailing wind direction.

The act of putting this sketch together will give you a solid orientation to the yard itself, before you begin planning any changes. When you have completed your map, put it aside for a while.

Planning your outdoor spaces involves considering not only how the yard might be redesigned but also how the house itself may be successfully incorporated into the new design. In this multileveled outdoor scheme, both the house and the yard are used to create distinctly separate areas for entertainment and recreation.

The next step is for you and the members of your family to generate a list of all the purposes you want your outdoor property to serve. Start by dreaming. Visualize how you imagine using the yard and jot down the images you get. Assuming you want to be able to relax in your yard, you may conjure up a picture of yourself lying in a hammock, holding a cool drink in your hand, and watching birds hop around a brightly colored feeder. Maybe you'll imagine yourself taking a sunbath and listening to the sound of a waterfall. Maybe you'll see yourself in a hot tub, or a treehouse, or a garden bower.

It's important to take this fantasy approach at first so that you won't eventually be disappointed by how your yard turns out. It tells you what you really want, regardless of possible restrictions. It can also help you settle on a principal theme or quality that you'd like to incorporate into your yard as a whole, whatever the final features may be.

Consider all your hobbies and habits

This low-lying garden was planned so that it can be viewed from several elevations.

17

and how the outdoors may accommodate them. Think about how and whom you have entertained in the past and how you'd like to entertain in the future. Gradually you can become more practical, concentrating on ways to move clutter outside the house or to engineer a more efficient driveway.

Once you have assembled a list of everything you'd like to do with your outdoor property, sort the individual ideas into functional categories such as "entertaining," "spaces for children," "recreation," and "gardens." Then take each category and establish priorities. Weed out or modify the items that do not satisfy these priorities. Work out ways to combine similar items.

The final step in your preliminary planning is to assign functional areas to different outdoor locations on your sketch. You may want to draw these functional areas on transparent sheets that can overlay your sketch, so that you can conveniently make several possible designs.

Ask yourself general questions and

Left: This indoor-outdoor entertainment space is highly efficient and yet it incorporates several stylish elements. The wall-mounted screen, for example, allows for a constantly shifting pattern of light and shadow, which offsets the stark lines of the surfaces around it.

Given only a small outdoor space, this homeowner used wood cleverly to fashion a combination entertainment-recreation-garden area.

record your answers in broad strokes. Which area or areas of your backyard are most suitable for entertaining, given the ideas you have generated? Which spaces are most suitable for children, given both your ideas for children's spaces and the areas you've carved out for entertaining? Which areas are most suitable for recreation? For gardens? When you've answered these general questions, you can go on to draw in details relating to each of the functional areas you've marked.

Bear in mind that you can change or remove some of the property elements shown on your original sketch to allow for a better plan; for example, you may want to cut down a straggly tree that blocks a good view and a natural traffic route or tear down a utility shed that occupies land better suited for a garden. You can also set aside single areas for multifunctional use—an open yard, for instance, that lends itself to both entertaining and recreation.

The value of taking a functional approach to mapping outdoor spaces is in giving your overall plan a cohesive, dynamic, and flexible design. Individual features within functional areas can be added, altered, eliminated, or replaced as the needs and desires of you and your family evolve. Suppose that you definitely want a swimming pool, for example, but it isn't practical to build one for sev-

eral years. Following a functional property design, you can reserve space for the pool with some other easy-to-adapt recreational feature—like a graded surface for badminton and volleyball—and not worry about having to completely rearrange your plan when it's time to install the pool.

What makes a functional outdoor design both practical and attractive is the natural grace it brings to your living environment. Instead of just surrounding your house, your land has a purpose and a vitality that can't help but communicate beauty and style to you, the members of your family, and your guests.

Facing page: *A generous expanse of level lawn—framed by trees, shrubs, plants, and fencing—can be a place for you to entertain guests, for your children to ramble, and for the whole family to enjoy outdoor games.* Above: *This smoothly modulated garden provides a relaxing view from both indoors and outdoors.*

CHAPTER TWO

GETTING OUTSIDE HELP

You've dreamed about what you want outdoors. You've made a lot of notes. You've even drawn up a plan. This doesn't mean, however, that you are ready to run out to the nursery, pool supplier, plant store, or lumberyard.

Once you've got a firm grip on your own ideas, it's time to test them against the legal and natural limitations affecting your property. It's also time to get expert advice about the costs, resources, and time frames associated with the individual projects you've envisioned. And, finally, it's time to see if anyone else has some better ideas for helping you achieve the general goals you've set for your outdoor spaces.

THE LAW AND THE LAND

Local building and zoning codes can have a profound influence on what you can and can't do with your yard. They can dictate easement restrictions (that is, how close you can build to public property), drainage patterns, fence and wall heights, and the design, size, and proximity to the house or property line of any permanent outbuildings. They can also contain regulations governing pools, septic tanks, and other underground features that may affect either public health and safety, local land stability, the water table, or power, water, and gas lines.

In many areas, utility company representatives will advise you, free of charge, about where their lines and pipes lie and public engineers will conduct free soil tests to determine whether your ground is strong enough to bear the weight and interference of any structures. You may also want to see if your property is recorded in a plat—a scale drawing prepared by a professional surveyor—on file with your local government. It will clear up any confusion about where, precisely, your property ends and other private property or public land begins.

CHOOSING AMONG LANDSCAPE PROFESSIONALS

Many people who are quick to consult an expert when they are planning their indoor spaces balk at consulting an expert when they are planning their outdoor spaces. The most probable reason for this is not that the outdoors is any easier to design. On the contrary, the average person knows much less about nature than about the artificial environment of rooms and furnishings, and mistakes outdoors are liable to be much more costly and time-consuming to correct than mistakes indoors. Most likely, people resist the notion of hiring an outdoor-design expert simply because they are not sure what kind of help is available and how best to utilize it.

There are several different kinds of landscape professionals that may be

Above: *Achieving an attractive mix of colors, textures, and shapes in your garden space often requires the input of a professional who is trained in aesthetics as well as in the limitations of climate and soil.*

Left: *It may be best to subcontract masonry work like this expansive stairstep complex. You can add your own personal touches later.*

Below: *This fairly sophisticated juxtaposition of a red brick patio, an oversized piece of dark green latticework, and a host of different plantings represents the kind of stylish touch a landscape architect can give to a yard.*

able to assist you. Ranging in order from most highly trained to least, they are known as landscape architects, landscape designers, landscape contractors, nurserymen, and gardeners. Deciding which professional—or combination of professionals—best suits your needs is a matter of understanding their different qualifications, capabilities, and modes of operation.

A *landscape architect* is a licensed professional who has had at least four years of formal schooling in landscape architecture, including studies in horticulture, art history, engineering, geology, biology, and meterology. In most areas, he or she must serve an additional four years of apprenticeship to a practicing landscape architect and pass an exam in order to qualify for the license. Landscape architects are skilled in doing everything from creating a general design for your property that is both practical and aesthetically appealing to drafting specific plans for each facet of your outdoor remodeling. They can offer competent, reliable advice on contouring your land; constructing and siting buildings, walls, patios, decks, pools, courts, and sewage lines; and selecting trees, shrubs, flowers, vegetables, furniture, and sculptures to put in your garden.

A *landscape designer* may perform any or all of the functions of a landscape architect but he or she is not a licensed

Left: *Many nurseries display sample flower arrangements to assist homeowners in planning their gardens.* Facing page: *Large nurseries furnish everything from seeds and seedlings to fully mature plants.*

professional, which means there are no legal requirements attached to the title. The typical landscape designer's studies are specialized in horticulture, and large nurseries often have several designers on their staffs. A common scenario is for a client or a landscape contractor to hire a landscape designer solely to provide aesthetic input into not-yet-completed outdoor plans.

A *landscape contractor* actually executes an outdoor plan, whether that plan is drawn up by a landscape architect, a landscape designer, or the client. Landscape contractors are frequently independent agents with their own crews, who can hire landscape architects or landscape designers if the need arises. They are capable of acquiring all materials and performing all earth-moving and construction tasks. There are no legal requirements regarding their education or qualifications.

A *nurseryman* traditionally raises plants both for wholesale distribution to landscape contractors and for retail sale to the public at large. Nurserymen can also be landscape architects, landscape contractors, or landscape designers. In some cases, especially if the nursery itself is a big one, nurserymen will employ a full range of landscape professionals to serve their clients. In other cases, nurserymen only recommend professionals.

A *gardener*, also called a *landscape gardener*, generally has no formal training at all, but his or her working experience may be substantial. A gardener's expertise lies in choosing, installing, and maintaining plants. Most often gardeners are hired on a year-round basis, their job being to nurture gardens and keep them in good repair.

WORKING WITH PROFESSIONALS

Developing an effective strategy for using landscape professionals to help you realize your outdoor plans requires self-assessment plus detective work plus common sense. If your plans are relatively modest and you're confident about them, you may want to do most of your outdoor work yourself, hiring a contractor or a laborer to perform some of the more difficult tasks. On the other hand, if your plans are ambitious and you're not sure how to implement them, you may be happier hiring a landscape architect to take care of the entire job.

Most strategies for redesigning outdoor spaces fall somewhere in the middle of these two extremes. Assuming you just want to make sure you aren't about to do something foolish or too costly, you can hire a landscape architect by the hour to review your plan, offer advice, and recommend a good contractor. Maybe you'll want an architect or designer to come up with a complete set of plans and then you can take over, acting as your own contractor and parceling out individual tasks to subcontractors.

A good way to help you decide how and with whom you want to work is to look for local domestic outdoor spaces that you like and inquire about how they were designed and built. The owners of those spaces are bound to be flattered

This yard has one very distinctive feature — a water lily pool — that required the services of a landscape architect and a contractor.

A delicately balanced design that encompasses an entire yard, like this Japanese-style rock garden, needs to be executed by experienced professionals.

This lovely patio structure was devised by a professional to fulfill many functions. It conceals and protects serving equipment, increases the privacy of patio users, and serves as a focal point that balances the mass of the house.

by your interest. You can also check with friends, relatives, realtors, nurserymen, and local consumer agencies. If all else fails, you can look up professionals in the phone book.

As a preliminary step to securing bids, find out current prices for the materials you imagine using in your outdoor spaces so that you can compare these prices with the costs quoted in estimates submitted by the architects, designers, or contractors you interview. Take detailed lists of all possible materials to building-supply houses, nurseries, lumberyards, and pool manufacturers. You can also ask the employees at these places for their recommendations about outdoor construction tactics and what kinds of professionals to hire for various jobs. Then get bids from at least three different architects, designers, or contractors and analyze and compare them carefully before making your final choice.

Negotiating services with a landscape architect is fairly straightforward. The contract you eventually sign is a standard legal agreement used by everyone in the profession that spells out what is to be done, what the fee will be, how payments will be made, and what the responsibilities and liabilities of each party will be. Among the responsibilities of the architect may or may not be supervising the contractor, according to your wishes. An agreement with a landscape de-

Left: *A customized fence adds liveliness and vertical interest to an otherwise conventional yard design.* Above: *This neatly tailored herb garden is the product of a collaboration between a do-it-yourself homeowner and a nurseryman who suggested specific plants.*

31

Below: *An imaginative treatment of rocks rescues a terrain that can't easily support a lawn or a wide variety of greenery. Professional skill has also been exercised in the judicious placement of hardy plantings.*

Above: *The sinuous perimeter of this elegant, dark-tiled pool reveals how a professional's touch can bring glamour to any site. The limited garden space is made imposing by a densely packed assortment of contrasting shrubs and trees.*

Below: *Just the right combination of design, materials, and setting makes this swimming pool triumph over the basic smallness, unevenness, and boxiness of the lot itself. Such components as the stone retaining wall and the peninsular tree-planting basin demanded experienced engineering input.*

signer can be modeled on this standard contract, which any nurseryman can tell you how to obtain.

Negotiating services with a contractor is more complicated, since there is no standard form to use. Make sure that any contract you sign contains these very important features:

- a detailed description of all tasks to be performed;
- an exact list of all materials to be purchased along with their costs;
- a statement concerning how any extra charges will be determined;
- a clause specifying that the contractor will obtain all needed permits and certificates;
- a clause requiring the contractor to arrange for any needed inspections;
- a statement that insurance for all laborers is to be provided by the contractor as required by law, including workmen's compensation and general liability;
- a statement that the contractor is liable for any property damage due to the work itself;
- a statement that the contractor must make all provisions for hauling away debris;
- a statement articulating the method of payment and dates of payment;

Architectural features that help prevent erosion and the resulting collapse of plants, ground surfaces, walls, fences, and outbuildings are essential on most properties that have grading variants exceeding six degrees. Here a tri-level wooden structure—shown before plants were added to the troughs—is expertly contrived to be both visually pleasing and eminently supportive.

Above: *An appealing, natural-looking cascade of wood-framed tiers doubles as a staircase and a means of erosion control. Each tier has been precisely sized and shaped for maximum safety and effectiveness.*

Right: *For this deck built around two trees, the homeowner enlisted the services of an architect to draw up the plans and material specifications. The labor involved in putting the deck together was relatively uncomplicated, so the homeowner did this part of the work himself.*

Every aspect of this yard—from the substantial gazebo to the rail fence and surrounding foliage—is part of a single grand design.

- a list of completion dates for each major task as well as for the entire job.

Ideally, you want a contractor who is able to provide a performance bond, which ensures that you will have funds to retain other contractors to complete a job in the event that the signing contractor fails to do so for any reason. The normal method of paying a contractor is never in advance but in increments as the work is done: for example, one-third of the total amount when one-third of the work is done, one-third when two-thirds is done, and the remaining third when the job is finished. Usually the homeowner agrees to provide liability insurance that protects the contractor's equipment and personnel while carrying out the work. The homeowner also provides property insurance protecting the entire work site and all materials from fire, vandalism, and malicious mischief.

Most jobs big enough to require a landscape contractor actually call for the services of several contractors such as masons, carpenters, and electricians. In this situation, the landscape contractor is the general contractor, with whom you have a legally binding agreement, and the other contractors are considered subcontractors, with whom the general contractor makes separate, legally binding agreements.

If you want to function as your own general contractor, you need to be very proficient at sequencing tasks among your various subcontractors. If you are not good at this kind of scheduling, it's best to leave it to a professional. A better way to become more involved in the work—so that you can cut expenses and oversee what's happening—is to agree to do part of the work yourself, especially simple, labor-intensive tasks that are costly, such as nailing deck boards to a frame or installing tiles around a pool. Then you are technically a laborer "hired" by your contractor.

A final consideration when it comes to seeking outside help in remodeling your outdoor spaces is to investigate possible government assistance programs and tax credits. You may be able to get a subsidy or a tax deduction, for example, by including an energy-saving solar collector in your plans or by using a swimming pool or garden pool as a solar device. Under certain circumstances, farm assistance programs provide free fish for ponds or free soil-conserving bushes for gardens. Check all the options with your local planning board and agricultural agent as well as in appropriate government publications.

Creating this ingenious, house-attached enclosure for a pool and a hot tub involved some research into the neighborhood's building codes as well as extensive input from a landscape architect.

PART TWO:

DESIGNING BY FUNCTION

CHAPTER THREE

ENTERTAINING

Throughout human history, people have relished entertaining guests in the outdoor spaces adjoining their homes. The ancient Greeks, who believed that conversation and food had more flavor in the open air, hosted friends and relatives on stone terraces attached to the backs of their residences. The household atrium—an interior courtyard—was a popular social retreat during the days of the Roman Republic and Empire. Even the patrician senator Cicero remarked that people felt more at ease with each other "under the sky, where rank and privilege are less meaningful." In the Middle Ages, increasingly elaborate pavilions and enclosed garden areas for outdoor parties celebrated humankind's taming of the wilds and mastery over the elements. By contrast, the popularity of al fresco dining in the last two centuries apparently reflects a desire to escape civilization and recommune with nature.

The sheer number of reasons why people enjoy outdoor entertainment suggests one of the most distinctive characteristics of the outdoors itself: its capacity for variety. In the fresh air, each hour that passes has its own look and feel, which makes every gathering outdoors a unique and especially memorable occasion. Even more to the point, the same outdoor landscape, with a little human ingenuity, can become an appropriate backdrop for any social activity under the sun or the moon, from a formal reception for fifty, to a family barbecue, to a romantic picnic for two.

PLANNING A ROOM IN THE OPEN

The main element in most outdoor entertainment plans is a sizable patio or deck—a clearly defined ground space that offers a strong, easily maintainable surface for people and furniture and, if desired, walls and overhead structures. Regardless of how the finished product looks or works, two basic principles apply. First, in order to be as versatile as possible, a patio or deck needs to adjoin or be very near the house itself, preferably in the path of the largest flow of traffic. In most cases, this means that the patio or deck will serve as an extension of the living or dining room. Such an arrangement provides convenient access to shelter and to such entertainment "support systems" as the kitchen and the bathroom. Second, in order to be as aesthetically appealing as possible, a deck or patio needs to create a smooth transition between the architecture of the house and the architecture of the land.

Before you begin drawing up plans for this outdoor room, consider your past patterns of entertainment. What types of gatherings have you typically hosted? If you do a lot of business entertaining, you may prefer the formal look of a flagstone patio to the more rustic look of a wooden deck. What times of the day and the year do you most frequently entertain? If it is

Bright canvas awnings and latticework help unify a series of separate entertainment spaces.

Above: *This serene patio, like the greenery that surrounds it, owes its charm to an ingenious mix of rustic materials and clean, elegant design.* Above right: *Lights strewn casually among the branches of an overhanging pine add a touch of fantasy to this utilitarian deck and lath structure.* Bottom right: *Decorative wrought iron columns and railings blend beautifully with plants to give this outdoor space a pleasingly natural-looking design.*

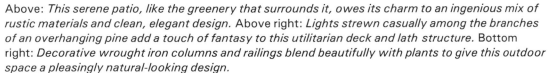

A low, brick plant trough neatly ties together the brick wall of the house and the brick-colored pavers.

apt to be cold, windy, or rainy during these times, you will want to include suitable shelter in your designs. How many people do you need to accommodate? Since an individual requires approximately twenty square feet to be comfortable (a four-by-five-foot area allows for one chair and room to circulate), parties for an average of twenty people suggest a patio or deck that is roughly four hundred square feet. Do you want to be able to separate children and adults? This may mean establishing distinctly different entertainment areas. Are many of your guests elderly? If so, you will want to provide very firm footing and eliminate unnecessary steps and barriers.

PATIOS

A patio, or inlaid surface cover, is a uniquely adaptable concept. As long as the ground extending from your house is basically flat (no more than a six-degree slope), and the earth itself is permeable and stable (a mixture of rock, sand, and silt rather than all sand, clay, or topsoil), you can choose among numerous attractive patio designs featuring different sizes, shapes, and materials that will not only expand your home-entertainment space easily and unobtrusively but will also harmonize beautifully with your property as a whole.

Patios are most commonly made of brick, concrete, stone, or pavers. Brick is especially popular because it comes in a wide range of colors—from yellow ochers to deep browns—and can look either earthy or refined, depending on the brick itself, the pattern in which it is arranged, and the manner in which it is mortared or secured in the ground. In cold climates, brick is especially vulnerable to destructive frost heaving, so it may not be the most practical alternative in these regions.

Concrete offers the most flexibility of any material in terms of shape. Although some homeowners are quick to discount a concrete patio as too institutional in appearance, many concrete aggregates, which consist of cement mixed with small stones, are quite handsome besides being very durable and easy to maintain. Concrete can be easily dressed with wood stripping (possibly the forms themselves in which it is poured) that provides visual appeal and pulls double duty as expansion joints, keeping the concrete from cracking during freezes or thaws. It can also be broom-finished; carved to simulate flagstone; stamped with designs, such as a brick pattern; or treated with a variety of coloring compounds.

Stone is nature's own flooring and is highly valued as a patio material. Flagstone—stone that has been cut flat on two sides—is expensive and relatively difficult to install, however it can provide a

The flagstone used in the support walls, stairs, and surface of this patio is the unifying element.

Above: *A border of flower beds mediates well between a brick wall and a flagstone surface in this semiprivate patio. Shrubs and trees behind the wall soften the sharp changes in the wall elevation. Facing page: Allowing grass to grow around the flagstones of a patio smoothly connects it to the surrounding greenery. In the photograph to the immediate right, carefully clipped grass creates an appropriate trim for the straight-edged flagstones in a formal patio. In the photograph to the far right, a shaggier trim complements a rougher, more primitive patio design.*

very attractive patio surface. Individual flagstones can be fitted together in mortar for a contoured look or placed randomly in mortar for a more open-ended pattern. A flagstone patio has the advantage of being able to look as formal or as informal as you please, depending on your particular design.

Pavers are blocks or tiles, usually made of concrete, that are manufactured in various tints and interlocking shapes expressly for patio construction. Some even have individual surface designs that can combine to form an interesting mosaic. Most, however, resemble bricks or stones. Pavers retain a fresh look for many years

and a patio made of pavers is easy to repair or extend.

The simplest and most sensible approach to patio design is to first consider the dominant style and shape of your house and yard and work toward reflecting these qualities in your patio. A Georgian house surrounded by carefully tailored garden beds, for example, calls for a correspondingly elegant patio: perhaps a brick patio of a strict rectangular shape with a low wrought-iron fence around the perimeter. If the style or geometry of your house and yard differ, a patio can function as a pleasing transition between the two. In the case of a boxlike, all-glass house on a rocky, partially wooded lot, an irregularly shaped patio of dressed stone—mixing both natural and utilitarian qualities—may be the perfect solution.

A more complicated tactic is to design a patio that offers a refreshingly provocative contrast to the style or geometry of the house and yard. Attaching a rustic brick patio to a contemporary house of poured concrete with a small, grassy yard may provide just the right amount of warmth and drama for effective outdoor entertaining. This design strategy can backfire, however; if you follow it, be sure you fashion detailed drawings and mock-ups of your patio and its surroundings before beginning any construction. These drawings should also be shown to several professionals to ensure their viability.

The same considerations that affect the design of your patio surface also affect any aboveground additions to your patio. To secure either visual, acoustical or psychological privacy, or to provide shelter from wind, or to screen views of raised play equipment such as swings and sliding boards, you may want to add fencing or walls to your patio. Depending on your overall design scheme, such an element may be a row of planters, a raised planting bed around two sides of the patio, a trellis at one end, or an encircling stone wall that doubles as a bench for seating or placing food and drinks.

An overhead structure can offer shade during the daytime and, possibly, shelter from the rain as well. Many patio owners prefer to go inside when it is raining, so the overheads they choose are open lath-work attached to corner posts or extended from the house roof to break the intensity of the sun. Some patios are built deliberately around nearby trees for shade purposes. For those who like the open-air quality of a lath structure but prefer to stay outside when it's raining, rollable coverings such as canvas or Saran shade cloth can be conveniently installed at one end of a lath structure. For those who desire more secure protection, glass, fiberglass, or plastic panels

Three different but harmonious lattice arrangements give overhead visual excitement to this patio.

are durable translucent roofing materials that are easy to mount on a lath shelter. An egg-crate pattern of laths can carry more than one type of infill: some openings can be covered with wood, others with plastic or screens.

DECKS

A deck is a crossbreed: It is part porch, part patio. It stands above ground level and is specifically geared toward making the best of sloping or poorly graded yards. Most characteristically of all, it is constructed of wood.

Its attractive woodiness is a major reason why a deck is an increasingly popular choice for outdoor entertaining. Wood blends well with almost any natural landscape and it can be as nice to touch and smell as it is to see. There is also an undeniably homey and companionable aspect to wood that soothes the spirit and puts people in the mood for relaxing. A large wooden addition, however, may not suit the design of your house. If you live in a chateau-style house, for example, you may have to forego your dream of a wraparound redwood deck, or else design some wall treatment to camouflage the deck after it is built.

Very often a deck is attached to a

Above: *This wooden deck is integral to the shingled saltbox house it surrounds. A smooth extension of the roof links the two entrances and provides shelter and shade for deck users.*
Left: *A hollowed log and tree stump converted into planters, a railroad tie used for bench support, and wooden columns are used as decorative accents to enliven this utilitarian deck. The bedroom balcony directly above the deck is constructed of the same materials in a similar pattern.*

Left: *The trunks and crowns of living trees mix with the supports and roof of an overhead lath structure to create a uniquely hospitable deck space. The indoor-outdoor balance subtly links the house with the outdoor pool.*

Facing page: *This deck-stairs-landing complex is successfully tied to the house by a beautifully proportioned railing, stained to match the building's trim and shingles. The horizontal lines in the steps and lower side of the deck interplay with the vertical rails to echo the building's rectangular design motif.*

tween the house and the yard, harboring much-needed storage space, or concealing the ruins of a hard-surfaced patio. Occasionally, when it can't be anchored on the site, a deck is cantilevered from the house itself and gives guests the sensation that they are suspended in midair.

Decks can not only unify different ground levels, they can also create them, whether they are attached to the house or freestanding. Multileveled decks furnish separate areas for conversation, dining, or game playing. A deck above a patio is a spot where adults may separate themselves from young children and still supervise their play. If you have a large, impressive tree in your yard, perch a deck on posts encircling the trunk and you have a sophisticated tree house.

Like patios, decks are more frequently convenient for entertaining guests when fencing, either with or without overhead structures, is included to provide privacy and protection from the elements. The best of these are wooden and casual in design, like the principal structure. But if the deck is close to the ground, a low bordering wall of brick or stone may not only look lovely but also help to relate the wood of the deck to other materials in your home or property.

A deck more than two feet above the ground needs to have some sort of rail-

house at floor level and thrusts outward to provide a level surface where a patio cannot because the ground itself slopes downward from the house. Sometimes a deck extends from a higher story and includes a substantial stairway, for example, in a house built on a hillside where the first floor in the front becomes the second floor on the back. Other times it rests on level ground just a foot or two below the floor level of the house, functioning as a pleasing transitional element be-

One of the main functions of a well-planned deck is to control outdoor traffic, so that you, your family, and your guests derive maximum benefit from the available outdoor space. Facing page, far left: *One deck narrows into a walkway to another deck, reserving space for decorative ground cover in between.* Left: *A sloping wooden ramp offers a dramatic entrance to this rooftop deck.* Above: *An intricately fashioned, multileveled deck creates distinctly separate areas for cooking and dining, hot-tubbing, and gardening.*

ing to prevent accidental falls, and many deck owners have cleverly arranged for both safety and seating by fashioning built-in benches with back supports around the sides of their decks. A trellis acting as a wall or a roof can support greenery that will lend charm and color to a deck. A more elaborate lath or post-and-beam structure mounted on a deck can lend security while giving the appearance of an outdoor parlor.

SHADE STRUCTURES

Gazebo, pergola, arbor, pavilion, ramada, lath house: Whatever their individual distinctions, all are essentially the same thing—a freestanding, roofed structure without solid walls that offers respite from direct sunlight. Usually such a shade structure is intimate in scale and serves as a focal point for a particular area of landscape that is well removed from the house itself. There is almost always a floor covering, either similar to that of a patio or deck or a much less finished surface of shredded bark or gravel. Often the roof is sufficiently covered to furnish adequate shelter from rain as well as sun.

A gazebo (the word originated in the Victorian Age as mock-Latin for "I shall see") is an especially decorative shade shelter typically consisting of five, six, or eight sides topped with a peaked roof. The most appropriate ornamentation

Perched on a slight elevation for good viewing and cool breezes, this large octagonal gazebo makes a perfect outdoor living or dining room.

The side trim of this pergola gives it a delicate, serene quality reminiscent of Japanese architecture.

depends on both the setting and your personal entertaining style. A gazebo can be sublimely primitive, with partial walls of braided twigs and branches and a conical thatched top, or supremely ornate, with elaborately carved scrollwork along posts and beams and a shingled roof featuring shallow gables.

As its name implies, a gazebo is a place for admiring the views on all sides, so it is best situated on a high grade or amid luxuriant plantings. It makes a wonderful romantic retreat for tête-à-têtes during large parties or for small, informal lunches or teas with close friends.

The word "pergola"—like the words "pavilion," "lath house," and "ramada"—refers to a rectangular post-and-beam construction closely resembling the kinds of overhead structures that are attached to patios and decks. This type of shade structure is generally both larger in size and simpler in design than a gazebo.

A pergola is especially practical when you are using your entire yard to entertain large groups of people. It can be a place to set up a buffet table, a bar, or chairs and tables for those who wish to enjoy a more private atmosphere away from the house. A pergola looks especially inviting when it is either shrouded in vines or bushes or topped with an attractive, easily replaceable covering such as a mat of woven reed or a canvas cloth in festive colors.

COOKING FACILITIES

The main value of eating outdoors is being able to escape the confines of the house—the walls that block views and keep people apart, the trapped air that can quickly grow stale, the carpeting and furniture that can block traffic and be so easily soiled. How liberating it is if you can not only serve food outdoors but also cook it outdoors!

If you rarely have large parties, your yard space is limited, or the season for outdoor activities is short, a portable cooking facility may be more practical than a permanent one. Portable units for grilling and heating food are available in a wide assortment of sizes and styles, from hibachis that sit comfortably on even the smallest decks or patios; to circular charcoal grills that can be wheeled anywhere in the yard; to large carts with propane grills, warming pans, storage shelves and counter space that can be stationed in a semiprivate spot away from the main body of guests.

A permanent installation, however, usually functions far more effectively as a substitute kitchen, plus it can be a handsome structural addition to your property. Would-be outdoor chefs who have a sizable brick, stone, or cement patio often prefer attaching a fireplace oven and grill of the same material to an upwind corner of the patio. This way they can be close to their guests and to the house it-self, where the food is stored.

Many hosts choose instead to locate a masonry fireplace further away from the house in a more secluded area of the yard. Such a fireplace may vary from a two-foot-high permanent grill mount of rough fieldstone to an elaborate eight-foot-high complex of ashlar stone or intricately laid brick containing a built-in grill, a ventilation hood, warming and baking ovens, storage cabinets, and counter space with cutting boards.

More serious cooks go one step further to construct a fully operable kitchen unit with sink, running water, electrical outlets, refrigerator, electric or gas burners, grill, and oven. Frequently this kitchen unit is housed in a compact hutch-and-deck structure with roofing that will shield the cook from sudden bad weather and allow for free air circulation. When the cook is finished, the hutch can be easily and securely closed off. Similar constructions are equipped as outdoor wet bars, especially when near a pool or outdoor spa.

A simpler, yet more dramatic, cooking alternative is the fire pit—essentially a hole in the ground for burning wood or coals, lined with firebricks, and incorporating a raised rim to hold a portable grill and a safety cover. A fire pit surrounded by flooring and movable benches or chairs has all the coziness of a campfire, even when you aren't cooking anything.

Left: *This easy-to-construct fire pit is safely attached to a far, downwind corner of a deck that has been treated with fire retardants. Its circular shape is mirrored by the shapes of the outdoor shower and hot tub on the other side of the deck.* Above: *This handsome, portable electric barbecue grill can be used in the garden by simply plugging it into an extension cable connected to the nearest socket.*

Ultimately, the tone of an outdoor space is established by its furnishings. Above: *Heavy, well-crafted wooden furniture with water-resistant cushions gives this outdoor space the formality of an indoor living room.* Facing page, top left: *Rustic garden chairs complement a natural-style patio.* Facing page, bottom center: *Ample cushions resting on low-lying lounge platforms lend a welcome touch of comfort to this spartan patio.* Facing page, top right: *A simple wooden bench provides seating space without detracting from the pleasing lines of the wooden arbor.*

gle items of furniture will best fulfill each of the possible usage circumstances I anticipate? What style of furniture will be most compatible with the surrounding property?

The most enjoyable aspect of the outdoors is its spaciousness. For this reason, most experts advise homeowners to keep the amount and bulk of outdoor furniture to a minimum. Make two lists of your furniture needs based on the kinds of entertaining you plan to do in your outdoor space. One list should be entitled "indispensables" for items that will be consistently needed; the other list "optionals" for items that will be needed only

It is also like a campfire in other respects—you need to make sure that local regulations permit open fires and that you situate the pit where smoke will most often drift away without troubling guests or neighbors.

FURNISHINGS

Few industries have grown as rapidly in the past ten years as the outdoor furniture industry, and the result is a bewilderingly vast array of chairs, benches, lounges, tables, and carts on the commercial market. In order to narrow down your choices, you need to ask yourself three questions: How much space am I willing to take up with furniture? What sin-

occasionally. The former list may include entries like "seating and table space large enough for family plus four friends," "four lounge chairs," "service cart to move between barbecue and patio." The latter list may include entries like "seating and buffet tables for a party of sixty people."

Make sure to acquire first-list items that are durable enough to withstand continual use and to be left outside permanently. You may prefer to rent or borrow "optionals" as needed; or you may choose to purchase second-list items that are demountable, stackable, or much more streamlined than equivalent first-list items so that they are easy to

tures can perform double duty. A series of steps leading to a deck or a low masonry wall protecting a patio can be designed to function effectively as places to sit during a large gathering.

The best way to ensure that your outdoor furniture complements the overall style of your outdoor space is to select individual pieces that can be directly linked by material or design to the environment. Built-in furniture, such as a cedar table that extends across one corner of a cedar deck, is an obvious example of this design principle. Examples of more subtle applications are a bench encircling the trunk of a big shade tree, a duckboard table on a concrete patio trimmed with wooden strips, cushion covers with a crisscross pattern for a chaise under a trellis, or tubular steel and textured glass shelves against a cooly elegant brick wall.

Careful advance planning pays off not only in creating large areas for social gatherings but also in choosing furniture to inhabit those areas. In fact, your guests may be far more sensitive to your furniture than to any other aspect of your outdoor entertainment space. When it comes to making final furniture decisions, give plenty of thought to the comfort and convenience of the people who will be visiting you and to the overall image you want to project as a host, whatever the occasion may be.

Left: *This rough-hewn stone bench fits well with the shaggy hedge, tall grass, and clover in its environment.*

Facing page: *This pergola becomes a romantically stylish retreat with the help of a muslin curtain, mirror, and wraparound seating in a dramatic green-and-white color scheme.*

move, space efficient when used, and convenient to store.

Look for furniture that satisfies a multitude of purposes. Cubes of varnished hardwood may serve as chairs, tables, or plant stands. A wrought-iron bench can provide seating for three party guests or, with the aid of a thick pad, can act as a lounging platform for a single sunbather. In some cases, structural fea-

CHAPTER FOUR

SPACE FOR CHILDREN

Children instinctively lay claim to the outdoors as their domain by natural right. Inside the house, everything is a reminder of adult power—the scale of the rooms and furnishings, the procedures for keeping things clean, and the restrictions affecting noise and movement. Outside the house, the world offers equal welcome to living beings of all sizes and a much freer scope for self-expression. Here children can exercise their minds as well as their bodies, giving full rein to their life-sustaining and life-creating talents of make-believe and imagination.

SELECTING PLAY SITES

Inevitably, children will roam all over the yard if there are not barriers to delineate play areas. You will be wise to consider this fact when you begin planning your outdoor space as a whole. What areas do you want to keep free (at least some of the time) from the noise or intrusion of children, such as a flower garden or a patio where you frequently entertain adults? How can you protect these areas? What potential hazards exist in the outdoor environment, such as dangerous ravines, rocky or marshy land, busy streets or driveways, or a neighbor's dog-run? How can you minimize these hazards? What potential areas for play exist in the outdoor environment, such as paved ground appropriate for bicycling or skating, a large tree that can support a swing or a tree house, or a gentle slope for rolling, sliding, and climbing? How can you direct the flow of traffic to lead children toward these desirable features?

Above all, kids prize wide-open space—room to run, to play tag, to do cartwheels, to watch clouds, to catch fireflies. With this in mind, many outdoor designs for households with children start with a large area of unobstructed lawn. Ideally, this functions as a natural living room that benefits everyone in the family. It's a place where children and adults can play together, using a rubber ball, an exercise mat, a portable lawn game, or simply their own wits.

Territoriality is also important to children. They need their own space outdoors as well as indoors so that they can develop a sense of independence and self-reliance. In addition to maintaining a large open area in your yard, you will want to reserve one or more smaller areas primarily for the use of your child—or children—and a reasonable number of playmates.

Right: *Children love to wander along interesting trails. This broad, rock-strewn garden is ideal, featuring hardy, widely spaced plants of different sizes, shapes, textures, and colors and a sturdy ground cover of gravel and wood chips.* Facing page: *An English boxwood maze is an endless delight for young children and their playmates. It stimulates their imaginations, encourages them to exercise, and offers private nooks for playing, thinking, or resting.*

You may wish to establish separate places for different types of play, for example, an area featuring a multipurpose gymnastic structure for strenuous physical exercises, an area surrounding a playhouse for quieter, more socially oriented games, and an area tucked out of sight where children can mess around with loose materials like tires, railroad ties, logs, wooden spools, and metal drums. This setup accommodates the changing desires of a child, depending on his or her daily moods or companions, plus it cuts down on the accidents that happen when two types of play occur in the same territory.

If you have marked off a large open play area in the center of the yard, you may want to position individual play structures and pieces of play equipment along the periphery in a roughly continuous line. The result is a maze of play options that stimulates a child's powers of creativity.

Whatever arrangement of play areas you choose, it's a good idea to provide some place where older children can enjoy privacy. They are bound to seek such a place anyway. Logically, it will be an environment that is conducive to more relaxed kinds of fun, such as a hideaway behind a hedge that invites daydreaming, chatting with friends, or reading a favorite book. You will probably want to be able to observe more vigorous activities from the house, especially if young children are involved. In this case, you can situate any structures or equipment that foster such play in a more direct line of sight.

EXERCISE STRUCTURES AND EQUIPMENT

When most people, both children and adults, think of outdoor play areas, they think immediately of commercial, ready-to-assemble swing sets, jungle gyms, slides, and teeter-totters. Living in a society that is intensely goal oriented, we tend to associate recreation with specific routines requiring specific paraphernalia. Unfortunately, parents who act on such tendencies may discover that the expensive aluminum athletic complex they have imposed upon their otherwise woodsy backyard is totally abandoned by their children after a few weeks of initial curiosity have passed.

When it comes to outfitting play areas, it makes much more sense in the long run to consider first what your kids enjoy doing, what kinds of activities will help them to develop healthy bodies, and how the landscape itself can be integrated with potential structures or equipment to create spaces that inspire enthusiastic and imaginative play. Children will do what they want to do on their own time, and that is usually not restricted simply to

No piece of play equipment is more popular with children than a swing. This simple arrangement doesn't interfere with the beauty of the lawn design.

This multifunctional wooden play structure helps children use their minds to develop their bodies.

Left: *A tire hung on a rope provides a number of play options, depending on how a child swings or twists it.* Facing page: *A strong, tightly meshed hammock can be enjoyed by both children and adults. It may even persuade a rambunctious child to settle down!*

swing or a metal spaceship climber—is irresistible to all family members and supplies a dash of color and drama to the overall outdoor scene. Because a child's interests and capacities evolve rapidly from year to year, however, the most practical exercise structures are those that consist of modular components that can be purchased individually and can be reassembled in more challenging forms as a child grows older.

Most forest-product companies manufacture an integrated line of versatile exercise devices that can be mounted around various styles of platforms, including ramps for sliding, rolling, and crawling; boards and teeters for balancing; and horizontal and vertical ladders for building arm and leg strength. All components are made of high-quality wood stock that has been sanded and beveled. Such pieces can be purchased unfinished, stained, varnished, or painted in bright, bold patterns.

what they can do on a specific piece of play equipment.

Observe your children during their leisure time in the yard. Note what kinds of games they like the most, how they make use of natural features in the yard, and what types of physical exercise they are currently unable to perform because of the limitations of the land. After you have collected a number of your own ideas, share them with your children and in-volve them in designing possible play structures and equipment, both on paper and with the help of three-dimensional modeling materials like clay, cardboard, and popsicle sticks. This will motivate your children to become more interested in utilizing, maintaining, and, eventually, upgrading their play areas.

Sometimes the carnival-like charm of a particular piece of commercial playground equipment—a fiberglass animal

The advantage of this type of system lies in its simplicity and flexibility. Its woody beauty and its abstract, sculptural quality make it a visually appealing element in the yard, and its functional diversity allows children to exercise their imaginations as well as their bodies. A platform can become the roof of a crawl space, a way station along an adventurous journey, or a jumping-off spot for a sliding pole. A beam can be lowered one month for balancing games, raised higher another month for chin-ups, and raised even higher the following month to serve as an attachment for a climbing rope or a swing.

Some parents and children prefer a much more modest approach to exercise structures and equipment, especially if yard space is limited. In this case, the adaptability of a single exercise unit to a number of different activities is especially advantageous. Climbing nets, made of sturdy ropes spaced widely apart and hung across a beam or a frame, suggest countless make-believe games that will assist children in developing muscular strength and coordination. Two tall, well-secured poles can be used individually for climbing or together to support a cable and pulley for gliding, a hammock for swinging, or a net for playing badminton and volleyball.

Whatever exercise structures and equipment you plan to use in your yard,

This attractive play structure is expansive and versatile enough to entertain several children of different ages safely and productively. Note the enclosed gravel ground cover—an added safety feature.

evaluate them carefully in terms of their safety and durability. Children are born risk takers—rough on themselves as well as their playthings. They need to be allowed to test themselves so that they can realize their abilities and limitations, but there are certain basic measures you can take to minimize accidents. Choose materials that are sturdy and require very little maintenance. Favor designs that are scaled to accommodate the size of your children—both now and over the next few years—and that have a minimum of sharp corners or joints. Locate individual structures and pieces of equipment away from potential obstacles (for instance, keep swings away from heavy traffic paths). Make sure the ground cover around each structure or piece of equipment suits the activity (for instance, sand or woodchips help soften the landing below a slide).

PLAYHOUSES

A playhouse is not just a place for kids to "play house." It is a magical setting for all sorts of adventures. Depending on the whim of the day, it can be a castle, a pirate ship, a fort, a store, a laboratory, a schoolroom, an office, a workshop, or a hideout. Whatever the imagination may make of it, a playhouse is also an undeniably practical feature in a yard used regularly by children. Here they can seek shelter from sun, wind, or rain. Here they can store toys and small play equipment. Here they can entertain company or relish their own solitude.

How much enjoyment children get from a playhouse depends a lot on how much they have to do with designing the structure. Some children prefer a very simple framework—such as two posts and a crossbeam, A-frame supports, or a geodesic dome—on which they super-

A blend of the playful and the sophisticated, this tree house is mounted on beams that run between two trees. The first story is level with a neighboring hill. The second story provides elevation with minimal worry of accidental injury.

impose a cloth or planks to fashion different kinds of room space. Other children prefer a more elaborate building, with finished windows, doors, and a roof deck. Among the issues to ponder together are how durable the playhouse needs to be (given the climate and the number of people using it), what design allows for the widest range of play options, and what construction style is most compatible with the surroundings.

If you have a large deciduous tree in your yard, give serious thought to the possibility of a tree house. Children live in a world of giants and tree houses offer them a psychologically refreshing change in perspective. The best site is a tree with a main trunk that divides into two or more major limbs that are about eight feet above the ground and that provide a minimum of three support points at the same level. In the case of a high-branching tree, you can do what the Kennedys and Carters did at the White House: build a tree-house platform that encircles the trunk and is set on free-

71

A freestanding platform provides the base for this treeless tree house. The peaked roof, deck, and circular entrance give it the appearance of a birdhouse.

standing posts. You can even construct a "treeless" tree house using four pillars or a single pole in conjunction with sturdy diagonal supports.

Any tree house requires special safety measures. Do not venture above eight feet high if small children will be using it. Do not build in trees that are near electrical or telephone wires. Avoid cutting into trees. Keep nailing or screwing into trees to a minimum—it is better, for example, to use a wooden, metal, or rope ladder for access to a tree house than to use steps attached to the tree, which can lose their strength. Set up mechanisms for convenient interaction with the ground—for example, a pulley system to lift heavy or bulky objects or a sliding pole to facilitate quick and smooth exits.

PLAY ENVIRONMENTS

The outdoor space surrounding his or her home is where a child first begins studying nature. An excellent way to encourage this learning endeavor is to provide environments where the child can manipulate natural elements easily, safely, and enjoyably.

A sandbox is a wonderful play space for a child's mind. Not only do kids delight in creating different designs and constructions out of the sand itself, they also enjoy inventing games and having lively

This marvelous movable tree house is available in kit form and is easy to assemble.

73

dialogues with their sandbox toys and companions.

Keeping a sandbox neat and comfortable, however, is a challenge. To avoid messy spillage, most effective sandboxes are either sunk well into the ground or include a generous lip around each edge, often slanted or half-cylindrical to permit sand to slide back into the box. They are also situated well away from strong winds and may have awn-

ings, shades, or covers. Since water frequently plays a major role in sand sculpture, a sandbox also needs to be well drained.

An attractive variation on the classic sandbox is the sand pit: a hole filled with sand that is bordered by cobblestones or flat paving stones. A series of steps leading down to the sand, or islands within the pit itself, can furnish handy places to sit or to mold.

Children may also welcome a manmade pond for lounging, wading, splashing, and exploring, especially in a hot climate. The pond can be lined with stones, filled by a hose, and drained after each use. Whether in use or not in use, a band of stone with or without water winding sinuously along a ridge on your land can be aesthetically pleasing in its own right.

Any distinctive natural feature of your yard has the potential to serve as the basis for a play environment. You can embed a slide or climbing posts in a long, gentle slope. You can turn a rocky corner into a stepping-stone game. You can trim, train, or enhance trees to provide natural rooms, for example, by taking advantage of branches that hang to the ground or by growing plants or vines alongside a tree to create walls. You can transform a garden patch into a wondrous maze of corn, sunflowers, and bean tents.

The most successful and satisfying way to plan outdoor spaces for children is to look to children and to the child in yourself for ideas. Sometimes you'll see that the space itself is more important to play than what might be put in it, so temporary features may be more appropriate than permanent ones. Sometimes you'll glimpse possibilities that the space doesn't offer in its current state: a secret spot you enter by a tunnel, a towering crow's nest that will let you view a faraway skyline. Whatever you envision, the final outcome is more likely to be something you have fun engineering and your child has fun utilizing.

Natural environments that appeal to children can be beautiful and useful from an adult point of view as well. Facing page, far left: *An eye-catching tunnel of greenery makes an excellent hideaway.* Left: *A vegetable garden in separate raised beds invites a child's close attention and makes it easier for him or her to tend individual plants.* Above: *An enchanting parterre garden organized around a sundial appears to have come straight from the pages of* Alice in Wonderland.

CHAPTER FIVE

▮ RECREATION

Not too long ago a backyard swimming pool or tennis court was considered an extravagance. This is no longer true today. Private outdoor recreation areas of all types are becoming increasingly popular among homeowners concerned with their physical fitness, especially as public or commercial facilities grow more and more crowded.

Whether your favorite exercise is doing laps, slamming shots, dunking baskets, or spiking returns, you'll be far more inspired to improve your performance if the means to do it are right in your own backyard. Admittedly, these activities take up a lot of space and a large permanent installation like a pool or a court is bound to have a dramatic impact on how your property looks. The way to meet these challenges is to give as much attention to aesthetics as you do to function. The life of the body and the life of the mind are inextricably bound. An outdoor facility that is truly regenerating is one that is pleasing to look at as well as to use.

SWIMMING POOLS

What could be more simple—and simply beautiful—in appearance than a swimming pool? A pool would seem to be the most flexible of all outdoor recreational facilities in terms of possible size, style, and location. Yet creating a pool involves accommodating a wide range of logistical, legal, and social restrictions.

The nature of the land on your property may dictate how you construct your pool. If

A simple slate pool surround relieved by well-spaced stones creates an unobtrusive link between the pool itself and the forest-like environment.

you want a below-ground pool and the soil is mostly composed of sand (not strong enough to bear the weight of the water) or stone (difficult to penetrate and slow to drain), you will need to excavate a section of your property that greatly exceeds the site of the pool itself and fill it with a gravel, sand, and silt mixture that can form a dense and stable support mass. If the water table is high or if you need to compensate for a sharply angled surface grade, the surrounding soil—in addition to the structure of the pool itself—needs to be even stronger. Realizing this, you may decide that a smaller pool or an aboveground pool is more practical or desirable.

Most local and regional building codes require that all swimming pools feature an enclosure: a wall or fence within a specified distance of the pool itself that can help prevent accidents. Other common regulations govern how close a pool can be to a road easement,

This sunken whirlpool also functions as a pleasant vista for patio users. The broad descending steps are attractive and allow bathers to choose their own level.

a property boundary, and underground power, water, and gas lines. Certain communities will not permit pool drainage in the public sewer system, so plans for a pool have to include plans for a leaching field or septic tank. Any one of these legal factors can influence the final design or location of your pool.

In order to make your pool a pleasant place for swimmers and nonswimmers alike, you need to place the pool where it will get a maximum amount of daylight,

be sheltered from wind, and allow for plenty of walking space with good traction and drainage along the entire perimeter. It is also wise to keep grassy areas at a distance from the pool rim, so the water doesn't become polluted with dirt and the lawn doesn't suffer chlorine burning. If small children will be using the pool, it's best for safety's sake to situate the pool close to the house so that the entire surface is within easy viewing range of a window. In order to keep the

peace with your neighbors, locate or screen the pool so that they won't be bothered by noisy swimmers and purchase liability insurance in case a visitor suffers an injury while using your pool.

However numerous the initial considerations and qualifications in building a pool may be, there is still plenty of room to dream and plenty of ways you can make your dream come true. You can choose among several different construction techniques and hundreds of designs, both for the pool itself and for the surround.

Assuming the land itself is reasonably stable, a pool can be lined easily and inexpensively with reinforced vinyl (which is available in both flexible sheets and precast forms) instead of the more costly cement poured over a wire mesh. This is particularly appropriate for a natural-

Wood is admirably suited to pool enclosures. Here it casts its outdoor spell on a pool complex that includes a bath-shower, a hot tub with removable cover, and plenty of seating space for bathers.

A tidy border of large rocks links this pool in spirit to the efficient bungalow-style house beyond it.

A lap pool and the playfully interactive deck spaces around it are proportioned to reflect the geometric shapes of the adjoining house. In keeping with the overall severity of the house design, the poolside furniture is restricted to a few lean pieces—the sole accent being a large rock.

looking pool that is free form in shape and edged with stones or rocks to resemble a forest pond.

Rectangular, oval, and circular pools match almost any style of house, but you may want to build something with a bit more flair. If you live in a country French- or Georgian-style house, a strikingly long and narrow rectangular pool that resembles a formal reflecting pool, or a Grecian-style pool—rectangular with beveled corners—would look very handsome. A kidney-shape or L-shaped pool would be more suitable for a ranch house, while a Roman-style pool—rectangular with semicircular bays at each end—would be the ideal complement for a house with a classical facade.

A pool can also be sculpted to match or act as a counterpoint to the exact countours of your land or the precise architectural shapes of your house. You may even want islands or peninsulas in your pool, lined with spectacular poolside seating as well as distinct areas for different types of water activity. The same results can be achieved by fashioning a complex of separate pools joined by canals or waterfalls.

Many homeowners who like swimming for exercise but have very small yards are taking a more strictly functional approach and turning to lap pools. One lane wide and as long as space permits (at least four body lengths), lap pools can also be tucked into a side yard if you would rather reserve your backyard for other uses.

An aboveground pool may be the only feasible kind of pool if your property is located on a steep grade or if the soil composition is highly unfavorable for a below-ground pool. It's also, however, a common choice of people who want a less geologically disruptive and less costly installation. Although you can't be quite as inventive with an aboveground pool in terms of its shape, there is a lot you can do in terms of the placement and surround to make it attractive.

POOL SURROUNDS, ENCLOSURES, AND CABANAS

Whatever the size or shape of your pool, the pool surround can work marvelously to integrate the pool itself with the site it occupies. Given thoughtful treatment, it ties together the materials and the scale of the house, the pool, the adjacent landforms, and any structures that occupy these landforms.

A predominantly wood residence, for example, may call for a wooden deck around part—or all—of the pool's perimeter or for wooden fencing that closely follows the outline of the pool. A deck rising above a patio surround could pro-

vide not only a semiprivate viewing and sunning space but also a pleasingly elevated mass to balance either a sloping landscape or a house with strong vertical lines.

An aboveground pool set in a wooden deck, especially if the pool itself is built into a hillside or approached from the

second floor of the house, can have the same appearance as a below-ground pool. The combination deck and pool can also offer a pleasing elevated vista to those who use it—a vantage point for observing a large garden or a faraway landmark. Another way to lend beauty to an aboveground pool is to nestle it

among plantings or to camouflage the sides with fast-growing vines.

Your pool may require partial or total enclosure, depending on the overall aesthetic of your backyard design, your desire for privacy or reliable year-round use, and local climatic conditions. A wall that harmonizes well with the walls of your house can serve as a windbreak (louvered, pierced, or screened so that it doesn't create an overriding wind tunnel), a source of shade (a solid surface that casts a big shadow during the hot afternoon hours), and a viewing shield that, for example, protects the visual serenity of a formal garden or prevents pool users from having a direct view into nearby bedrooms or bathrooms.

You may want to encase the entire pool area in a climate-control structure that will permit comfortable swimming even when it is prohibitively cold, rainy, or windy outside. A rigid frame enclosure, which usually consists of spans of aluminum or steel that support inserts of glass,

This cabana, evoking colonial Williamsburg, serves as a pleasant counterpoint to its streamlined environment.

Plexiglas or plastic, can be designed in almost any shape and can be equipped to provide the same sort of atmospheric heating and cooling that exists inside your house. Several enclosure manufacturers market modified greenhouses that serve as attractive pool houses; some even offer rigid frames that can be rolled back on tracks built into the pool surround for times when the weather is nice.

A flexible, pneumatic enclosure is a portable apparatus that can be inflated reasonably quickly to offer pool shelter when days are rainy or windy. It also functions well in more temperate climates to extend the swimming season by two or three months, simply by taking advantage of natural solar heating.

If you aren't interested in enclosing your pool but want to have shelter from the open air, a cabana is the answer. Technically, the term "cabana" refers to a small room for changing clothes; but in common speech it has been used to describe any roofed poolside retreat, from

Covering more space than the pool itself, this multiroom cabana provides lots of options for entertaining guests and engaging in poolside recreational activities, regardless of the weather.

This cabana-and-pool complex is so carefully balanced and crisply styled that it resembles a shrine fronted by a reflecting pool.

workouts. You may want to transform it into a permanent social area with built-in seating and table space or a casual resting nook with collapsible chairs and lounges.

Above all, a cabana is a place for enjoying life; and this spirit is reflected in the way a cabana is constructed and decorated. Taking your cue from the environment as a whole, a cabana can assume the appearance of an exotic Arab tent, a thatched Samoan bungalow, a Victorian seaside pavilion, or a miniature yachting club. Like the water design itself, it can be as playful or as glamorous as you desire.

Top, left: *This homeowner decided to extend his house into the pool area with a pentagonal room specially equipped to support outdoor activities.* Bottom, left: *This cabana interior illustrates how a poolside structure can provide ample opportunity for colorful and imaginative interior design.*

SPAS

The pleasures and health benefits of soaking in hot water have been enjoyed for centuries; but only in the past twenty years, thanks to California-style hot tubs, has the outdoor spa become almost as popular as the outdoor pool.

Spas actually combine the functions of heat and massage and come in two basic modes: the hot tub and the whirlpool. Originally a wine vat, the hot tub is a prefabricated barrel made of redwood, teak, mahogany, cypress, cedar, or oak that is four to seven feet in diameter and seats up to six people. The whirlpool, by contrast, can take any shape or size and is made of metal, acrylic, fiberglass, concrete, or a sand-and-concrete mixture called Gunite. Both the hot tub and the whirlpool are designed to submerge the sitting body in about four feet of heated water and contain hydrojets that pum-

a full bath-and-dressing-room complex to an open-sided lath structure.

The most versatile cabanas usually take the form of a rectangular deck with a solid roof, one or more lattice or lath walls, and a small, fully enclosed room at one end. The roof provides full protection from rain and sun. The walls permit refreshing air circulation but break up any heavy drafts. The room serves not only as a changing room but also as storage space for items that you want to keep dry and out of the way.

The deck space of a cabana has limitless possibilities. You may want to include a bar there, string up hammocks, or install exercise equipment for fresh-air

Resembling a cutaway stage set, this sheltered hot-tub nook offers lots of space for lounging.

mel the skin with water streams of various intensities in order to relax the muscles.

As a means of reducing stress, soothing aches and pains, loosening up after exercise, and stimulating blood circulation, a spa is unexcelled. As a social means of bringing a small group of family or friends closer together, a spa is unique. Ideally, it should occupy a secluded niche or alcove in your property—one that offers privacy, shade, protection from chilly breezes, and pleasant natural surroundings. A spa can even be concealed by raised planting beds or sunk into the landscape itself to resemble an ornamental pool in a sheltered part of a garden. If your entire property is in an isolated area, you may instead want to locate your spa in a more open spot to take advantage of a good view.

Often a spa will be incorporated into a swimming pool. In this way, both spa and pool can share the same filtration and

Left: *This ingenious swimming pool/hot tub setup finds its inspiration in nature. By making liberal use of natural woods, opening the complex to the adjacent garden area, and designing it for maximum use of sunlight, this homeowner has created a stunning and highly successful segueway to the out-of-doors.*

Facing page: *This freestanding wet/dry sauna is a perfect addition to a pool-side complex. Easy to assemble, this particular model comes with an interior faucet that can be attached to a garden hose or permanently plumbed to provide for steam. This sauna, with its red cedar planks, integrates nicely into a wooded backyard.*

heating system and water lovers can move back and forth easily between them. Spas are also frequently built in conjunction with a deck, in many cases on the top level of a multi-tier design. A major bonus of this set-up is that the spa can be covered with deck boards, enlarging the deck for other uses. Other spa owners, concerned about the vagaries of the weather, top their spas with plastic bubbles or house their spas in partial or complete enclosures.

TENNIS COURTS

For anyone who plays tennis, or wants to play tennis, a court of one's own has an incalculable value. It's a game in itself—and not a pleasant one—to secure convenient and sufficient court time at a tennis club or public facility; and the cost of this time grows with the demand. Having your own court means playing whenever and however you want in comfort and solitude. It is a powerful incentive for perfecting your skills as well as a magnet for attracting other people to play with you.

There isn't much room to be creative in fitting a tennis court into design plans for your outdoor space. The rules and conditions of the game are the greatest determinant of how your court will look and where it will be situated. The court needs to lie on top of subsoil that is easily drained (sand, sandy loam, or gravel) and be situated well away from structures or trees that might cast shadows across the playing area. The length of the court is best oriented from north to south to avoid having to play with the sun in your eyes. Preferably there would be a windbreak, such as a distant stand of trees or a grassy knoll, blocking the court from the usual direction of windflow and

Left: *Instead of surrounding his tennis court with ugly metal fencing to entrap wayward tennis balls, this smart homeowner chose to use a dense hedge.* Facing page: *This beach-side tennis court is picturesquely situated near the water and its cooling breezes to ensure maximum comfort when playing.*

a ten-to-twelve-foot backstop along the perimeter of the court to keep balls inside. Ideally, there would be a dark background at both ends of the court to make the ball more visible to each player.

As for the surface of the court, you do have a number of alternatives. Porous floors, which consist of vanishing (or vanished) grass, clay, or fast-drying compounds like crushed stone or brick, are easy to install but require a high degree of maintenance. Nonporous floors, which consist of concrete or acrylic-finished asphalt, are more complicated to install but require much less maintenance. An acrylic-finished asphalt court, for example, will last up to four or five years between refinishings and relinings.

A well-designed court made of high-quality materials is bound to please the eye of any tennis lover; but it may not harmonize too effectively with the other elements in your overall outdoor design. All things being equal, the best place to locate your court is away from the house in an area that is visually screened. This means freedom from distraction for both players and nonplayers. It also keeps the court itself, which is functional rather than ornamental, from dominating the backyard scene. Backstops come in many different designs—flat, curled, and wing shaped—and one of these may be particularly attractive for your property. You

can also try reflecting the proportions or colors of the court in nearby outdoor features, for example, in planting beds that frame the court area.

OTHER GAMES, OTHER SPACES

Individual households will have their own favorite outdoor recreation. You may want to include a putting green in your backyard, a small ice-skating rink, a basketball hoop, or a tetherball pole. If you don't have any specific sport in mind, however, or if your family likes different kinds of games, or if you frequently entertain friends who enjoy outdoor exercise in general, you may want to consider creating recreation spaces on your property that are suitable for a variety of physical activities.

The most adaptable game space is a large, open, level area of lawn. Here you can play touch football, set up a badminton or volleyball net, lay out a croquet game, pitch horseshoes, practice archery—even hold a mini-Olympics. Because this outdoor space may receive a lot of hard use, you may want to separate it visually, even acoustically, from the rest of the yard, either with a fence, plantings, or a shade-cum-storage structure.

Sometimes people will build a platform or deck for outdoor recreation, either because their land is not level or they wish to

confine noise and rigorous physical activity to a specific spot. A platform tennis court (also called a paddle tennis court) is one example of this strategy. So is an outdoor weight-lifting or gymnastics room. Typically these structures are surrounded by screening. Usually they are made of wood, but steel and aluminum construction is increasingly common, especially in climates where easy snow re-

For the dedicated croquet fan, a well-manicured playing field is a joy, despite the high maintenance involved. The close-cropped grass goes well with any outdoor design.

moval is an issue. Whatever the case may be, such recreational platforms and decks are designed for efficiency and are best kept out of view from the rest of the property.

A rectangular ground space of concrete or asphalt is wonderful for such pavement games as shuffleboard or hopscotch or for just bouncing and dribbling a ball, as children love to do. In many cases, this involves a simple extension of a driveway, which can mean additional parking space as well.

No matter how you design your outdoor space for recreation, individual activities are certain to spill over into the yard as a whole from time to time. With this in mind, there are basic safety and convenience factors that need to prevail throughout your property. Make sure that traction is good everywhere and particularly strong around areas of water or a change in grade. Choose appropriate night-time lighting for each region of your yard, giving special care to recreational spaces. Swimming pools are safest with lights around the coping; quartz floodlighting offers the best illumination for a tennis court; incandescent lighting works for a basketball hoop, and mercury vapor lights are effective for a large play area such as an open lawn. If you are comfortable and secure in your surroundings, you will get much more fun out of your play.

This backyard deck and cabana complex offers great motivation for working out.

CHAPTER SIX

▌GARDENS

In no other way do human beings and nature interact so perfectly as in the creation of a garden. From the initial planning of where and what the garden will be to the tending of the mature plants, homeowners develop a keen appreciation of the geophysical forces that shape the land they occupy: the soil, the sun, the wind, the humidity, the seasons. Nature, in turn, provides aesthetic enrichment to the homeowner's property and lifestyle: a showcase of colors, shapes, textures, patterns, and fragrances that enliven the yard and enthrall the senses.

A garden is a living entity. Given proper care, its beauty and character evolve slowly over the years. For this reason, a garden is best considered an ongoing project in your life outdoors rather than a fixed feature. It's important to give a great deal of thought to the location and basic structure of your garden plus its immediate and long-range future before purchasing a single plant.

To ensure the maximum amount of benefit from the time and effort put into a garden, it's best to strike a comfortable balance in design between your creative conception and the practical considerations of your garden environment. Also, allow room for change, so that you can recover easily from unforeseen problems, take advantage of opportunities, and accommodate shifts in personal tastes or needs.

Although it is well within the average homeowner's capabilities to plant and nurture almost any kind of garden, it's a good idea to seek expert advice in the crucial period of initial planning. It can save you a great deal of wasted time, costly mistakes, and

Above: *Large masses of marigolds and zinnias and the juxtaposition of a rough-textured rock against the smooth lines of a simple wooden bench make this ingenious garden both formal and exuberant.* Facing page: *A sinuous bed of red salvia leisurely directs traffic and attention to a picturesque gazebo.*

frustrating disappointments. Landscape architects or designers are professionally trained in horticulture and will be able to assess the garden potential of your land in a technical manner that you may not be able to duplicate on your own. More important, they have experience in visualizing season-by-season garden possibilities and in devising garden layouts that will highlight the strong points of your outdoor space and mask the weak points.

Once you've obtained qualified input concerning the design of your garden, you either can proceed on your own to establish the garden, or divide that chore into parts that you can do yourself and parts that a landscape contractor or a gardener could do. The first step of all, however, is to examine your own opinions and wishes regarding the garden in advance of seeking outside help. Only then can you determine if the ideas you receive from others adequately address your needs and desires.

PRELIMINARY CONSIDERATIONS

What is the chief virtue of a garden? It's lovely to look at. Beyond any other consideration, you want your garden to be visually appealing, and this means choosing individual plants that grow robustly and harmonize well with their sur-

roundings—both natural and structural. Planning your garden also entails creating a mix of plants that lends variety and beauty throughout the year.

It makes sense to situate your garden where it will offer the most viewing pleasure as long as this doesn't interfere with

major outdoor traffic patterns. Note natural focal points in your yard: the crest of a small hill, an empty sward of lawn fronting a patio, or a line of sight directed by the angle of a wall. Be sure to include outdoor vistas from inside the house in your thinking. In addition, investigate

your property with an eye to possible functional purposes. Maybe your garden could supply a special resting spot away from the house. Perhaps it could define the border between two separate areas of your yard, frame an entrance to the house, turn an oddly shaped side yard into a strong decorative element, or obscure an ugly view of a nearby commercial area.

Perhaps you already have in mind a particular purpose you want the garden to fulfill such as providing vegetables or herbs for home consumption or flowers for indoor arrangements. An increasing number of homeowners are now incorporating even more specialized and novelty gardens into their outdoor spaces. Among the more popular are edible gardens—the products of which can be plucked, rinsed, and tasted immediately—aquatic gardens, and children's adventure gardens, which contain a playful assortment of different types of plants as well as room for wandering and conducting planting experiments. In the case of deciding where to locate these theme gardens, your choices may be limited. They have to occupy the ground that promises the best conditions for their specific plant growth. With this in mind, you may want to develop alternatives for concealing such gardens or for enhancing the attractiveness of their setting.

After you've daydreamed for a while about where you want to put your garden and how you want it to look, it's time to approach the more mundane issues: the actual data concerning the topology, soil composition, and climate of your site that will enable you to determine what range of plantings will grow best in your garden. You may discover that your yard needs some remolding before cultivation—for example, to create better drainage gradients or to remove stony substrata. It could be desirable or necessary to build terraces that will support a garden along a slope or to utilize raised planting beds rather than the ground surface itself. Perhaps you'll want to replan a garden to include windbreaks or partial shade during the late afternoon.

Inevitably the plants that will look the best and require the least maintenance will be those that are native to your area of the globe. Nature works with a palette that subtly coordinates all the varied components of a particular region: the earth tones, the sky tones, and the colors of the flora and fauna. Even the shapes and textures of individual plants visually complement the environment that enables them to flourish without human intervention. You may want to use exotic plants to accent special features on your property, such as a pond or a sinuous front walk, or you may find that certain

A stairstep arrangement of stone terraces allows this gardener to create and harmonize a variety of separate mini rock gardens.

A tall, white backdrop emphasizes the unique sculptural qualities of cactus plants and very effectively dramatizes the sunlight upon which they thrive.

A maze of closely clipped hedges is a hallmark of the parterre-style garden. Here the empty space between plantings is as important as the plantings themselves. Right: This natural room-style garden frames a pergola and features corridors for viewing nicely balanced arrangements of achillea, foxgloves, and lamb's ears.

nonnative plants best suit your nonnative domestic architecture, such as bamboo to highlight a Japanese-style house in Virginia. In any case, devoting the major portion of your garden to native plants gives it the best chance of enduring indefinitely as a healthy and handsome addition to your land.

STYLE OPTIONS

Down through the ages since the garden of Eden, a number of distinct garden styles have been developed and refined to serve different situations. Whether or not you choose to recreate one of the major formal styles in your own garden, it is worth reviewing them to see how they integrate specific types of houses with specific types of settings as well as how they satisfy social and personal needs.

One of the most adaptable and elegant of all styles is known as the *parterre garden*. Characterized by strict geometric patterns that call attention to the ground plane, the parterre style was especially popular among the architects of seventeenth-century France who wanted to extend the precise lines of chateau architecture onto the flat landscape of the Loire valley.

The pleasure of a parterre garden comes from its orderly arrangement of horizontal features, such as planting beds, borders, walks, and lawns. The garden proper can be as intricate as a complex maze consisting of separate strands of flowers, each with its own distinct color, or as simple as a circular sweep of several monochromatic rows of a single type of flower.

The attractive symmetry of the parterre style works well when you want to outline a traffic route clearly, like a path to an entranceway, or when you only have limited space for a garden that will ideally possess strong viewing impact. The parterre approach also solves the problem of adding drama to a level site where contouring is inappropriate, or where heavy winds discourage vertical plantings and threaten the neat appearance of your garden. In areas that experience deep snow accumulation, a parterre design of low-lying evergreens can ensure that the garden maintains a discernibly clean structure all year long.

In contrast to the parterre style, the *natural-room style* works in three dimensions to give an outdoor space some of the cozy character of an indoor space. Many practitioners of this style actually employ trees, hedges, fences, or freestanding barriers to establish the same sort of vertical boundaries for their gardens that walls do for the rooms of a house. Inside these boundaries, interestingly varied groups and elevations of plantings not only invite observers to lin-

ger and refresh their senses but also create separate areas for them to inhabit. A cluster of shrubs in one corner makes a perfect retreat for reading. A corridor of roses, lavender, and salvia encourages a leisurely stroll. Decorative pots of palm strategically placed in a bower of Japanese maple form an enchanting backdrop for an impromptu picnic.

The natural-room style realized its purest historical expression in the atriums of ancient Greek and Roman villas and in the courtyards of medieval and Renaissance castles. Today, one often encounters this style in gardens that incorporate statues, sundials, fountains, pools, patios,

decks, or shade shelters. It's an ideal choice for gardens in which a lot of time will be spent performing diverse activities. It is also valuable in gardens where privacy is desired or where backyard space is limited and already partially enclosed.

Cottage gardens are filled with an abundance of flowers and are most appropriate for people who enjoy spending a good portion of their leisure time observing and tending their plants. The success of such a garden depends on combining different varieties of growth to achieve striking juxtapositions of color, texture, and design. To achieve this goal,

Facing page, far left: *An attractive rock garden such as this looks wild, but actually it depends on a subtle, carefully achieved blend of colors, textures, and masses.* Left: *Reveling in yellows, reds, and purples, this vibrant country garden almost overwhelms a romantic arbor.* Right: *The tranquility of this Oriental garden is ensured by bamboo screening.*

local soil and climate conditions need to favor the stable development of a sizable range of specimens. To complicate matters, the overall design of the garden is largely dictated by where individual plants have to be situated to grow the most effectively.

For many gardeners, these requirements add up to an exciting challenge: to cultivate a rich profusion of flowering plants that doesn't look like a chaotic freak of nature at one extreme or a botanical exhibit at the opposite extreme. The challenge is often met by selecting a basic theme for the garden that can govern and control plant selection. Famous examples of theme-oriented cottage gardens include the White Garden designed by Vita Sackville-West at Sissinghurst in Kent, which relies heavily on light-toned flowers; and the Unicorn Gar-

den at the Cloisters Museum in New York, which consists of plants depicted on the "Hunt of the Unicorn" tapestries. Most cottage gardeners, however, initially restrict themselves to a plan that involves only two to three different types of flowers or only two to three variations in color using the same type of flower. Throughout subsequent growing seasons, they experiment with new entries, retaining some and abandoning others.

A cottage garden takes up a lot of time and space; and although it can be fashioned to provide year-round viewing pleasure, it is bound to look better during some months than it does during others. Nevertheless, in full bloom it can be a matchless work of art; and in coming to produce that work of art, you can develop a relationship with nature that enhances your entire life.

In addition to the parterre, natural-room, and cottage styles, there are two other design options for household gardens that are less common but deserve mention. They are the *Oriental garden* and the *wild garden,* and they occupy opposite ends of the style spectrum.

The Oriental garden is a carefully contrived retreat from the active world, a place where simple forms and arrangements have a symbolic, abstract value that inspires passive contemplation. Individual plants, rocks, and ornaments are often carefully isolated to capture one's complete attention. The resulting minimalist effect appeals to homeowners who want their outdoor spaces to be practical and neat in appearance without looking empty or obsessively manicured. If the style of the house itself is not also relatively minimalist, however, an Oriental garden may look out of place.

The wild garden celebrates nature's exuberance. It appears to have grown spontaneously, unaided by human effort, though in reality it can demand almost as much planning and attention as any other type of garden.

The object of this garden style is to preserve all the existing natural features on the property and to enhance them by making small adjustments that do not interfere with the land's overall character. Rough paths can be added to lead wanderers to and from scenic spots. Patches of weeds can be replaced with patches of grass. Suitable flowers can be planted in an apparently random fashion where they might naturally grow. What is alien to the wild style are obvious indications of human tampering, like visible planting beds, cropped hedges, or wooden chips encircling tree trunks. A wild-garden style works well when the land itself is fairly expansive and contains numerous examples of raw natural beauty. If your property lacks much physical distinction or if it is surrounded by reminders of the civilized world, it is better to try a more tailored style.

SELECTING TREES, SHRUBS, AND FLOWERS

When it comes to determining which specific trees, shrubs, and flowers you want on your property, there are plenty of issues to consider regardless of whether your approach to garden style is formal or casual. Many of these issues are potentially minor ones, depending on your personal preferences. Are you willing to nurse plantings over several years before your landscape achieves its desired outcome or do you prefer plantings that will immediately give your landscape a finished look? Are you interested in growth that will repel insects and herbivores or attract birds? How important is fragrance to you? Do you want to coordinate the full flowering of your garden with a particular time of the year when you do most of your entertaining? What proportion of annuals, biennials, and perennials best fits your objectives?

There is one major issue, however, that is vital to the success of every garden. One must exercise informed judgment rather than personal inclination in deciding which individual plants possess the shapes, textures, and colors that are the most complementary in a particular garden site.

Beginning with trees and shrubs, the largest and most influential garden elements, you will want to create natural forms that balance the general character of the landscape. If it is a jagged or inclined landscape, trees or shrubs with a vertical silhouette are best—columnar evergreens or tall, narrow deciduous trees like the poplar. Horizontal trees and shrubs, such as spreading evergreens or

A border of bird-of-paradise plants dresses up a Moorish-style, stucco facade and serves as a counterbalance to the palm trees that tower over the corner of the house.

The brightly colored tulips, hyacinths, and daffodils at the base of this tulip tree lend dramatic appeal to the coverlet of fallen petals.

acacia trees, are ideal for a flat landscape. On a gently rolling landscape, the most suitable trees and shrubs are basically round, for example, spirea bushes or maples.

The shapes of trees and shrubs also need to be in harmony with the shapes of the house and any other major structure on the property. Where there is a conflict between the general character of the landscape and the appearance of the main residence, trees and shrubs can provide essential mediation. Assume, for instance, that you live in a Tudor-style house with several large, peaked gables that sits on a completely level lot. A smart choice for your principal trees and shrubs would be ones with broadly pyramidal shapes—possibly thick-based evergreens or pin oaks.

In selecting flowers, you can aim for a greater variety of shapes. Nevertheless, the best-looking gardens usually feature one dominant flower shape and use contrasting shapes as subtle counterpoints. Frequently the dominant flower shape mimics some significant detail in the surroundings. The bell-like shape of marigolds and tulips, for example, may blend beautifully with the shape of an adjacent rock, birdbath, or gazebo dome. Spires of hollyhock may pleasingly echo the lines in a nearby piece of lattice or deeply grooved tree trunk.

The basic rule regarding texture in trees and shrubs is that fine, thin textures look best in small areas and coarse, heavy textures look best in large areas. When it comes to flowers and ornamental greenery, the key concern is to avoid a chaotic mix of textures and strive for a soothing pattern of textural qualities that fits well with the surroundings. Finely grained mountain laurel set off by a bed of slick, glossy rhododendrons, for example, makes an attractive foundation garden for a house with large expanses of wood and glass.

The most outstanding aspect of any flower garden is color. A single vivid tone or a well-sequenced combination of tones injects new life into a landscape. Color can make a small garden look larger and more spectacular or tame a big garden by giving it a subtle complexion all its own. It can call attention to the best features in nearby buildings or foliage by restating their lines or hues. It can also compensate for drab or obtrusive elements by dressing them up or creating visual diversions.

Because color has this potency, it needs to be handled with great discrimination. Experts on the subject divide the color spectrum into three complementary pairings: red and green, orange and blue, yellow and purple. You will always get good results if you concentrate on one of these pairings, especially when you emphasize one of the paired

Given an imposing house situated on a large, open lawn, this striking specimen plant is the perfect accent.

colors and use the other color sparingly. For example, you could accent a bed of lemon-yellow lilies with violet asters, edge a rose garden with ivy, or play sparkling orange Oriental poppies against masses of cool blue delphiniums. An equally fool-proof color design is a garden that presents multiple shades of the same basic color, with the darkest shade or a pleasant contrasting color delineating the house from the garden.

VEGETABLE AND HERB GARDENS

Few labors are as gratifying as raising your own food on your own land. It makes little difference whether your goal is to continuously outfit a homegrown salad bar for eight hungry stomachs or merely to stock your bar from time to time with fresh mint. In raising a produce garden, you become intimately involved in the natural cycle of food production and you exercise the most fundamental of all civilized impulses—that of reaping practical benefits from the earth itself.

A vegetable or herb garden needs rich soil, a level surface with good drainage, and plenty of sun, so you may have little choice as to where to locate it on your property. You do have a great deal of choice, however, regarding the general appearance—including concealment—of the garden. In the eyes of its

A wide path allows this youngster to enjoy the wonder of a mature cauliflower without disturbing the rest of the vegetable garden.

Here vegetables and flowers meet in a meticulously groomed garden that is a pleasure to behold.

farmer, a vegetable or herb garden is always a beautiful sight; but to the outside observer, it can be a jarring interruption in an otherwise well-modulated and nicely functional outdoor scheme.

A vegetable or herb garden is essentially a parterre-style garden. Its formal arrangement of evenly spaced rows allows for maximum efficiency in plant growth and maintenance. Aesthetically speaking, this strong, basic pattern works in its favor, as long as all plants and the beds themselves are diligently tended.

Unfortunately, the garden is bare or thinly covered most of the year. If it occupies a highly visible spot on your land, you may want to alternate rows of decorative foliage or flowering specimen plants with rows of vegetables or herbs or create a clever arrangement of separate garden beds cut in shapes that are attractive even when bare. Terraced vegetable gardens look very handsome along a natural slope. Herb gardens can be trained to grow in fanciful designs know as "herb knots." Any style of vegetable or herb garden can be nestled within a smartly trimmed border of low-lying hedges.

Another option is to put the vegetable or herb garden out of sight, either by situating it behind a preexisting wall or building or by surrounding it with an enclosure of its own. Many homeowners block off a direct view of a garden with a shade shelter or a thick wall that includes convenient storage space for garden tools and supplies. Others use a strategically placed stand of trees or an open fence to provide a satisfying visual distinction between the garden and the rest of the property without completely hiding one from the other.

PATHS AND PERIMETERS

Walkways through garden spaces are practical additions that make it possible to take care of a substantial garden eas-ily and to enjoy in comfort all the sights it has to offer. They are also important outdoor design elements that have a major role in defining a garden's character and relating the garden to other parts of the property.

A path may provide strong, reassuring structure to a garden by encircling it or dividing it into an assortment of shapes that suits the landscape as a whole. This is particularly important if no other obvious feature, such as a natural border, a change in land elevation, a fence, or a wall attests to the logic of the garden's size or placement.

The material used to make the path can serve to link the house more closely to the land. The same wood, stone, slate, brick, or even aggregate concrete that forms part of the house exterior can be extended into paths that form the "bones" of the garden design. In some cases, an alternate material looks good in combination with the house materials. A path consisting of individual, neatly trimmed flagstones, for example, goes well with the precisely articulated brick facade of a Georgian-style house.

A path can also do a lot to highlight the atmosphere of a garden. A garden filled with small, cheerful wildflowers may be enhanced by a meandering network of narrow pressed-earth or gravel trails. Sealed oak rounds laid out as stepping stones may be the most appropriate path for a garden full of evergreens and tall, woody-stemmed flowers.

What is true of paths is true of walls and fences. Depending on their placement and composition, they can help give a garden definition and character as well as tie it more closely to the house and other major features of the property. Walls have the added functional capacities of offering privacy for garden lovers, support and background for various types of growth, and shade and shelter for humans and plants alike.

Solid walls or fences extending into the ground can actually impede the spread of frost to downstream plants, which may

Above left: *This brick wall and brick-lined path showcase flowering plants which might otherwise be overpowered by the surrounding trees.* Above right: *This lovely stepping-stone path showcases some spectacular azaleas and encourages garden viewers to take life a bit more slowly.*

Roses growing along a split-rail fence are well-suited to this unpretentious rural homestead.

lengthen their growing season. A solid fence, however, does not make a particularly good windbreak. The increased flow of air over the top can produce a cascading eddy that draws wind sharply back to the ground. A picket, slat, or louvered fence or an openwork wall will do a better job.

ORNAMENTAL WATER GARDENS

Water magnifies the charms of plants, and it's a relatively easy matter to incorporate bodies of water into your garden design. In many cases, you can sculpt a pool directly from the earth, line it with flexible vinyl, and edge it with rocks. If this isn't possible on your property, if you prefer a more polished look, or if you want an above-ground pool rather than a sunken pool, you have two alternatives. You can purchase a prefabricated fiberglass, plastic, or metal pool basin (prefabs are frost resistant and come in a wide range of sizes and shapes), or you can outline your own pool and cast it in cement over wire mesh. Once the basin is in place, you may create anything from a strictly ornamental reflecting pool to a sound-and-sight extravaganza filled with an assortment of sprays, waterfalls, acquatic plants, and decorative fish.

Most plants that grow in water are fairly hardy and do not require much atten-

tion, as long as the pool has been set up properly to accommodate them. Locate the pool so that is has at least three to four hours of direct sunlight a day. This fosters healthy plant growth and keeps bacteria down to an acceptable level. Any standing pool requires some degree of water aeration, which can be achieved by recirculating pumps, waterfalls, fountains, or periodic drainage and refill.

You may safely include fountains and fish in a pool with aquatic plants; but remember that while fish like turbulence, plants do not. Seek expert advice to make sure that you strike the right balance of elements. The shape and intensity of a fountain spray, for example, has a profound effect on the biology of a pool. You can control this effect by choosing the correct fountainhead to produce water domes, rings, bubbling streams, or jets.

GREENHOUSES AND COLD FRAMES

A greenhouse is an unique world of pleasure for serious gardeners. Aside from furnishing a tidy, private, ever-comfortable place where gardeners can indulge their interests, a greenhouse enables them to grow vegetables out of season, to raise exotic plant specimens under ideal conditions, to experiment with

Left: *An Oriental water garden makes a refreshing enclosed retreat within a large, woody lot.*
Above: *Here an entire lot is organized around an ornamental lily pond, which mirrors an elegantly sculpted bridge.*

113

Left: *This small, freestanding greenhouse is so attractively proportioned that it looks good right in the middle of the yard.*

Above: *This large, house-attached greenhouse is rendered a handsome backyard addition thanks to tapering wooden arches and a false flagstone floor.* Far right: *This house-attached greenhouse is partially camouflaged by a bed of sunflowers.*

crossbreeding and force-growing, to prepare seedlings for outdoor planting, and to pot outdoor plants for indoor decoration.

A *freestanding greenhouse* can also be a handsome structure on your property. Taking your cue from the style of your house and other outdoor buildings, you can erect a country greenhouse shaped like a barn with a gambrel roof, a Gothic-style greenhouse constructed with a longitudinal series of pointed arches, or a modern, basic A-frame greenhouse. You can use any number of transparent wall materials, from glass and acrylic—the most durable—to fiberglass and polyethylene film. You also have several different heating options to supplement the natural heat of trapped sunlight: gas heaters, electric heaters, or solar heat sinks consisting of barrels of water, rocks, or manufactured panels.

A *cold frame* is a glass- or plastic-covered box that sits over plants, keeping them warm and protecting them from the vagrancies of outdoor weather and traffic. They can be attractively designed as permanent fixtures in your garden or used occasionally for such temporary tasks as nurturing seedlings and covering flowers during a storm. A *hotbed* is a cold frame that is artificially heated. A *sun pit* is a cross between a greenhouse and a cold frame—a cold frame placed over a space carved out of the ground that is insulated by the earth and large enough for a gardener to work inside it.

The biggest advantage of greenhouses and cold frames is that they manage to combine the chief virtues of both the outdoors and the indoors. Throughout centuries of civilization they have done much more than give people greater opportunities for enjoying the outdoors. They have also offered people a means of fashioning their own outdoors in a magical indoor environment.

PART THREE:

PLAN INTO ACTION

CHAPTER SEVEN

SCHEDULING OUTDOOR PROJECTS

A scale drawing that meticulously details precisely what you want in each area of your property is wonderfully satisfying to contemplate. It represents the culmination of a major effort of imagination, research, calculation, and decision making. Holding it in your hands, you can get a tantalizing sensation that you already possess your new outdoor spaces. In reality, you have barely begun.

The most important and complicated aspect of planning your outdoors is scheduling an effective sequence of tasks for achieving the results you want to achieve. It's a logistical feat that requires you to visualize not just how your outdoor spaces will look when they are all finished, but how they will look at each stage of their development. It's time consuming, costly, and demoralizing to have to tear down a recently completed brick wall to create the proper grading for a garden, or to suspend the building of a deck until after the rainy season, or to endure a year as an unwilling hostage in the midst of construction-site chaos.

If you want to turn your beautiful drawing into a successful working plan, you need to be able to go beyond translating it into the three dimensions of space. You have to read it in terms of the fourth dimension of time. You don't want to be forced to destroy or disrupt work you've already done in order to begin the next phase of a particular project. You want to be sure that you have the right resources available—the time, the money, the equipment, and the personnel—to do each task when it's ready to be done. You also want to exercise as much control as you can over how well your property looks and functions during the process of remodeling.

118

As a help with how to sequence the tasks involved in creating your outdoor spaces, this chapter presents a sampling of time-related construction issues, organized according to the major functional areas discussed in this book. They are general, common-sense issues for the most part; nevertheless, they will give you some appreciation of how intricate the job of sequencing tasks in a big, outdoor make over can be and of how much the services of an experienced contractor may help.

ENTERTAINING SPACE

- You may not want to build a deck or patio until you've already created the view from that deck or patio or until all noisy and messy earth moving has been totally completed.
- If you want your deck or patio to encircle a tree or to include such built-in features as a fire pit or a spa, the tree or built-in feature must be securely in place before the construction of the deck or patio surface. The same rule applies to supports for any overhead structures likewise constructed.
- The piece-by-piece construction of a wall, fence, patio, or deck that follows the installation of the basic framework takes a great

Before this brick patio could be laid, the ground level had to be raised above protruding tree roots; otherwise, the patio would have suffered buckling from subsoil disturbance.

deal of time. You will want to coordinate this task with a season of the year when it's comfortable and convenient to work outdoors. If you are doing the task yourself, you may want to schedule it during a vacation time.

- If you anticipate the possibility of entertaining larger numbers of people in the future, you need to give thought to how you might eventually expand or supplement deck or patio space. This could require keeping a certain amount of your property in reserve.

SPACE FOR CHILDREN

- You need to project the future needs and desires of your children in terms of exercise and recreation. Some land may have to be kept in reserve for bigger and more elaborate play structures for your children as they mature physically and mentally. Specific needs and desires may be more efficiently met with temporary outdoor features (for example, an easily removable sandbox) rather than permanent features (for example, a stone-lined water-and-sand pit).

- Children never cease wanting to enjoy the yard, even during a construction process. You will want to organize individual building projects so that your children have a comfortable and safe play area at all times. If possible, you may want to schedule tasks that are especially disruptive to your yard—or that are disruptive to children's outdoor activities—for times when your children won't be at home all that much.

- It's wise to define and secure a general space for kids before outfitting that space with any structures or equipment. Depending on your plan, this could mean ensuring that the land itself is free of hazards and has good traction and grading; setting up fences, walls, and natural barricades; and installing lighting, walkways, and special play surfacings.

- The longer it takes to complete any construction in spaces for children, the more impatient the children get and the greater the risk is that they will wind up hurting themselves or causing damage to the project itself. Be sure you schedule these tasks so that they can be completed as swiftly and safely as possible.

RECREATION AREAS

- If you definitely want a swimming pool or a tennis court sometime in the future, you need to leave space for it, even as other projects in your yard take shape.

- If a pool is included in your current plans, you will want to make it your first project (after any land contouring) since it is apt to be the project that is the most disruptive to the environment as a whole.

- A pool surround should only be constructed after the pool itself is in place. If you want to locate a pool adjacent to an existing patio or deck, be prepared for the possibility of having to take it apart and rebuild it to accommodate the shape of the pool.

- If your long-range plans include both a pool and a spa, consider building them at the same time and coordinating their water-supply and filtering systems.

- In many areas, outdoor recreation is only practical during certain times of the year. To make the most out of a limited recreational season, try to schedule the construction of outside recreational features so that they're ready when the season comes.

Facing page: *Here the pool was built first, its design complementary to the lines of the house. The deck swings out over the pool surround, providing easy access and viewing pleasure.* Above: *Vertical supports for this spa enclosure needed to be sunk before the steps and platforms were constructed.* Right: *The spa and pool in this backyard were built simultaneously so that the water mains wouldn't have to be dug up twice.*

GARDENS

- It's usually best to postpone work on individual gardens until all land contouring has been completed and all major adjacent structures (such as walkways, fences, and walls) are in place.
- Most plantings work best if they are done at a particular time of the year, so that they can take root and grow under the most propitious weather conditions. Different types of plants may have different ideal planting seasons.
- There are definite advantages to having a garden in place before building a structure from which the garden will be viewed; however, you may have to weigh these advantages against the potential damage to the garden that the dust and activity of such a construction may cause.
- You will need to determine how long you're willing to wait before your garden has a finished look. You may want to plan a plant mix that will allow your garden to appear full and beautiful immediately, even though it may be a number of years before the garden as a whole reaches its planned maturity.

Facing page: *A window box in full bloom can provide visual interest during times when an adjacent garden may not have yet matured.* Left: *This flagstone path was laid before the garden was planted to ensure that no root systems would be disturbed.* Above: *Movable planters let you position high-impact specimen plants in temporarily bare or underdeveloped garden spots.*

CHAPTER EIGHT

PRACTICAL AND DECORATIVE ACCENTS

Once you start giving time and thought to improving your outdoor spaces, you set in motion a creative energy that never stops. It keeps you continually on the lookout for ideas that will increase the beauty, convenience, comfort, safety, and utility of each of the functional areas on your property.

This chapter discusses some of the ways you can embellish and enhance your basic outdoor design, either before it is executed or afterward, as new wishes and needs arise. It is hoped the suggestions offered here will direct your attention toward significant details—those objects and treatments through which you can add a distinctive personal touch to the environment at large.

LIGHTING

With a little imagination, a low-voltage lighting system can transform a nighttime landscape into a glamorous stage set. Small lamps concealed by greenery can guide footsteps along romantic paths and highlight the major attractions of your yard. They can make small gardens appear spacious and large gardens appear intimate. They can also accent the three-dimensionality of the landscape and its structures.

Contour lighting involves situating two or three lamps—each projecting a focused beam—around the periphery of the feature you want to illuminate, so that the beams strike it at different angles. As the name implies, contour lighting dramatizes objects that

already possess noteworthy sculptural qualities, like statues, big specimen plants, and trees. One beam needs to be markedly stronger in intensity than the other or others in order to produce a sufficiently sharp contrast of light and shadow. Experimentation is the only way to determine which angles and intensities work best in a particular site. You may want to vary the lighting arrangement every now and then, to suit different occasions or seasons.

Grazing is a technique of brushing light across a surface to emphasize its texture. It's a particularly effective means of illuminating a stucco, rough brick, or ivy-

Above left: *This finely modeled yard lantern looks beautiful whether it's lit or not.* Above: *An imaginative outdoor lighting scheme serves as both a work of art in its own right and as an essential safety feature, making it clear at night where the entrances, steps, and pool rim are.*

covered wall. If you want to bring out the shape or shapes of an artfully designed object—such as a statue, a topiary shrub, or a lattice fence—you can try *back-lighting, up-lighting, down-lighting,* or *cross-lighting* (this is when two equally intense light sources are mounted directly opposite each other on either side of the object).

The secret to a good lighting scheme is to avoid overlighting, particularly when you are using focused beams. Keep the intensity just bright enough to provide nighttime security and to display the color and form of interesting outdoor features. Avoid using tinted lights, which can unpleasantly distort the sizes, shapes, and hues of surrounding objects. Choose lamp settings that hide the fixtures themselves and eliminate unwanted glare. Devise any necessarily stronger, task-oriented lighting so that it's strictly confined to the task area and can be easily dimmed or turned off when no longer required.

Instead of contour or focused-beam lighting, you may prefer diffuse light emanating from an eye-catching source—one that complements the dominant theme in your outdoor design, such as a wall-mounted railway lantern, or a Victorian lamp post, or a tiki torch stake. This kind of lighting endows a large, heavily trafficked yard area with both safety and striking beauty.

STORAGE AND UTILITY AREAS

It's a fact of life both indoors and outdoors: The longer you inhabit a place, the more dependent you become on good storage and utility areas.

From the start of your outdoor planning, you need to take this fact into account. If you want a pool, you'll also want a convenient means of storing pool accessories and maintenance equipment. If you want a garden, you'll also want a handy location to keep tools and fertilizer. If you want a playground for kids, you'll also want a nearby spot where they can store their toys. You may even want entire spaces devoted to nothing but storage or utility: a secluded yard where you can dry clothes, pile up firewood, build a compost heap, store the lawn mower, or place the trash cans.

A basket of vibrant red geraniums atop a wooden beam and the adjacent planting dress up a woodpile and give it a unified design.

This miniature log cabin suggests whimsy more than the utility it actually offers.

No matter how farsighted your original plans are, however, you're certain to develop additional storage and utility needs as time passes. Then you're faced with the task of creating new storage and utility areas or redesigning existing ones so they serve you more efficiently.

Above all, it's important to remember that a storage or utility area is not merely a place where things sit around. It's an activity center as well. People come and go and move items back and forth. In designing storage and utility areas, give careful consideration to the traffic patterns associated with the functions they serve and to the physical build and capabilities of the people who will be using them. A modest building to store gardening paraphernalia, for example, may be much more practical if it is near the garden and contains a foldaway counter where gardeners can sit and mix liquid nutrients, pot plants, or arrange flowers.

The main conflict affecting storage and utility areas lies in how to make them attractive as well as serviceable. The most common solution is to conceal them. Small yard areas and buildings can be hidden behind hedges or walls. Storage compartments can be situated underneath the surface of a deck, beneath the hinged seat of a bench, or within a raised planting bed. A shallow locker to hold bicycles, firewood, or lawn-care products can be constructed along one wall of the house or the garage so that it blends in with the architecture as a whole.

An alternative is to devise storage and utility structures that are aesthetically pleasing in themselves. Custom-crafted wooden boxes can cover trash cans. A whimsical turn-of-the-century seaside dressing-room can resourcefully contain pool-cleaning apparatus. A playhouse can feature multishaped boxes built into an outside wall that are pleasing to the eye and good for stashing games, toys, and sporting equipment.

FENCE AND WALL TREATMENTS

Many outdoor spaces include solid, blank fences or walls that can be greatly enlivened with just a little ingenuity. One approach is to give the fence or wall an additional purpose. Use it to support a shelf of plants, or a game board, or a festive roll-up awning, or a handsome lean-to that can furnish shelter, privacy, or storage room.

A more artistic approach is to change the superficial appearance of the fence

Left: *The heaviness of this stone patio wall is much relieved by the colorful overflowing flowers on top.* Above: *A topiary arcade prevents the relatively severe house facade from dominating the garden.*

or wall. Add decorative molding to outline it or divide it into more intriguing shapes. Paint a boldly colored mural across it. You may opt for a scene that is in keeping with the basic theme of your outdoor design or for a tromp l'oeil composition that can give the space around the fence or wall a refreshing depth of perspective. Set a trellis in front of it to create intriguing shadow-and-light patterns. If it's a masonry fence or wall, train ivy to grow directly across the surface.

ART OBJECTS

Any property can benefit from an outdoor sculpture, provided that it is well chosen, well situated, and well mounted. The most promising sculpture is one that reflects the style, scale, and materials of its environment. A large house, incorporating geometric forms and materials like concrete and steel, for example, requires an outdoor sculpture that is also

large, geometric in form, and made of either concrete or steel or both. By no means does the match have to be this precise to succeed. If, for example, the sculpture is to be situated near a small, wooded corner of the grounds, it may be equally appropriate for it to be smaller and more naturalistic in design and material. Whatever the case, the sculpture needs to be positioned somewhere that is a focal point in its own right: a pleasantly framed part of the lawn, a turn midway between the house and the pool, a knoll just outside a living-room window.

You may derive even more pleasure from an outdoor work of art that is in some way functional as well as ornamental. A sundial, for example, can be a functional and yet beautiful centerpiece for a flower garden. A smartly arching bridge can be a lovely outdoor sight plus offer a novel viewing platform, regardless of whether or not it spans a body of water. A gigantic stone turtle can be a handsome climbing and resting place for kids, and for adults who are kids at heart.

Facing page, far left: *The vibrant azalea blossoms clustered around this concrete sundial produce an interesting contrast of colors and textures.* Left: *Juxtaposing two sculptures that appear to interact with one another injects drama into a limpid backyard vista.* Below: *These concrete urns filled with agave provide the needed eye-catching detail in a yard of monumental forms.*

ANIMAL HABITATS

A mixture of flora and fauna on your land truly qualifies it as a natural kingdom. The animals that are most common to domestic property are dogs and birds; and while dogs and birds are almost always fun to watch, they can potentially wreak havoc unless you plan your outdoor spaces with an eye to controlling their activities. Fortunately, you can do this and at the same time invest your yard with added visual attractions.

The things that can be done to dress up a dog run are admittedly limited. First, the run should be well proportioned, with hardy ground cover. Second, it needs to be placed away from those areas of your yard where you entertain and from those areas of your neighbors' yards where they spend a lot of time. Finally, it requires a visually unobtrusive enclosure that the dog can't penetrate, climb, or leap over. Faced with such restrictions, it's a good idea to surround a dog run with a

Facing page: *To enclose a pet yard for a rambunctious Irish setter, a homeowner with a small lot needed a fence that was tall and strong. This fence of square lattice frames attached to brick pillars satisfies those requirements without looking massive.*

Right: *Delightfully whimsical yet practical and durable, this wooden doghouse was custom made for its dalmation inhabitant.*

Below: *This dovecote nicely echoes the lines of the house.* Right: *A Chinese pavilion birdhouse adds color and ornament to an unadorned corner.* Below right: *Situated in an Oriental garden, this thatched bird feeder was inspired by Japanese shrines.*

solid wall or fence and then plant vines, a tall hedge, or a row of shrubs or trees to soften the effect of the lengthy barrier. This natural growth may also increase the acoustical insulation of the dog run.

Whether your dog has the freedom to move all around the yard or is confined to a specific yard area, think about acquiring or constructing a beautifully designed doghouse. It can be both a shelter from sun, wind, and rain for your pet and an appealing outdoor novelty. Some people prefer a doghouse that restates the architectural style of the main house; others prefer a doghouse that has its own distinctive style—one that suits either the dog, the landscape, or a personal whim.

Birdhouses, bird feeders, and birdbaths can be as delightful to the eye as birds themselves. Be careful, however, that the house, feeder, or bath you select is designed to draw the types of birds that you will enjoy and that will cause the least disruption to your life outdoors. You will want to avoid attracting birds that are very noisy, that eat plants, that bore deeply into trees, that scatter a lot of seeds, or that produce noisome and corrosive droppings.

Hung from a tree, houses and feeders can balance the impact of colorful plants or structures that lie closer to ground level. Freestanding houses or feeders lend charming vertical accents to flat or gently rolling landscapes, especially when they articulate the boundary between two different yard areas or a turning point in a traffic path. Many homeowners prefer placing houses or feeders near a window so that visiting birds can be observed both from indoors and outdoors.

In the case of an animal habitat or any other item that serves as a graceful note in your general outdoor design, be sure the component materials are strong, weather resistant, and easy to clean. This kind of object is intended to capture the viewer's attention; and so the impression it makes has a disproportionately strong influence on how the viewer regards the yard as a whole.

At once whimsical and stylish, this birdhouse lends focus to the entire corner of the backyard.

▎SOURCES

HOT TUBS AND SPAS

Almost Heaven Hot Tubs Ltd.
Route 219 North
Renick, WV 24966

Aquarius Baths Ltd.
211–215 West 20th Street
New York, NY 10011

California Cooperage
Railroad Square
Box E
San Luis Obispo, CA 93406

California Hot Tubs
60 Third Avenue
New York, NY 10003

Cecil Ellis Sauna and Leisure Corporation
99 White Birch Road
New Canaan, CT 06840

Gordon and Grant
423 North Quarantina
Santa Barbara, CA 92109

Jacuzzi Whirlpool Bath Company
298 North Wiget Lane
Walnut Creek, CA 94596

1129 Bloomfield Avenue
West Caldwell, NJ 07006

McLevy Products
1 Lefrak City Plaza
Elmhurst, NY 11368

National Equipment Manufacturing
Corporation
4655 118th Avenue North
Clearwater, FL 33520

San Diego Hot Tubs
960 Grand Avenue
San Diego, CA 92109

Spas Electera
13470 West Greenfield Avenue
Milwaukee, WI 53005

Vico Products Manufacturing
Company Inc.
1808 Potrero Avenue
South El Monte, CA 91733

The Wooden Tub
765 Felton-Empire Road
Felton, CA 95018

SWIMMING POOLS

Allied Pools
7351 North 76th Street
Milwaukee, WI 53005

Ames Manufacturing and Distributor
10004E South Memorial Parkway
Huntsville, AL 35803

Aquarius Pools, Inc.
West 2028 Sinto
Spokane, WA 99220

Bosco Industries
1308 Cook Street
Columbia, SC 29203

Coastal Industries, Inc.
P.O. Box 363
Carlstadt, NJ 07072

Dotts Corporation
1309 30th Street NW
Canton, OH 44709

Fort Wayne Pools, Inc.
510 Sumpter Drive
Fort Wayne, IN 46804

Hallmark Pool Corporation
2785 Algonquin Road
Rolling Meadows, IL 60008

Heldor Industries Inc.
1 Corey Road
Morristown, NJ 07960

Ideal Pool Corporation
3955 North Peachtree Road
Atlanta, GA 30341

Lane Swimming Pool Consultants
Foot of Cropsey Avenue
Brooklyn, New York 11224

National Spa and Pool Institute
2111 Eisenhower Avenue
Alexandria, VA 22314

National Swimming Pool Institute
2000 K Street NW
Washington, DC 20006

Pleasure Pools, Inc.
2180 Maiden Lane
St. Joseph, MI 49085

Polly Pools, Inc.
1401 North C Street
Sacramento, CA 95814

Polynesian Pools
905 Brooks Avenue
Holland, MI 49423

Pool Country
1863 Summit
Dallas, TX 75206

Purex Pool Products, Inc.
P.O. Box 1237
La Puente, CA 91749

Seaspray-Sharkline, Inc.
431 Bayview Avenue
Amityville, NY 11701

Swim Industry Corporation
1505 South Missouri Avenue
Clearwater, FL 33516

Weatherking East, Inc.
Route 130 & Cedar Lane
Burlington, NJ 08016

Wonder Industries
1813 Country Club
Paragould, AR 72450

WOOD PRODUCTS
(DECKS, FURNITURE, FENCING, STRUCTURES)

Aikenwood Corporation
2151 Park Boulevard
Palo Alto, CA 94306

American Plywood Association
1119 A Street
Tacoma, WA 98401

American Tack & Hardware
25 Robert Pitt Drive
Monsey, NY 10952

Baker Manufacturing Company
P.O. Box 28
Columbia, PA 17512

California Redwood Association
617 Montgomery Street
San Francisco, CA 94111

Century Family Products
3628 Crenshaw Boulevard
Los Angeles, CA 90016

Clairson International
5100 West Kennedy Boulevard
Tampa, FL 33609

East-West Design Inc.
Box 6022
Madison, WI 53716

Georgia-Pacific Corporation
133 Peachtree Street NE
Atlanta, GA 30303

Jer Manufacturing, Inc.
7205 Arthur Drive
Coopersville, MI 49404

Kenmore Industries, Inc.
Woodbine Road
P.O. Box 155
Belmont, MA 02178

Louisiana-Pacific Corporation
1300 SW Fifth Avenue
Portland, OR 97201

National Plan Service
435 West Fullerton Avenue
Elmhurst, IL 60126

Parrott Industries
44 Alco Place
Baltimore, MD 21227

Southern Forest Products Association
P.O. Box 52468
New Orleans, LA 70152

Western Wood Products Association
1500 Yeon Building
Portland, OR 97204

GREENHOUSES

Aluminum Greenhouses, Inc.
14615 Lorain Avenue
Cleveland, OH 44111

American Leisure Industries
Box 63
Deep River, CT 06417

Casa-planta
9489 Dayton Way
Beverly Hills, CA 90210

Ickes-Braun Glasshouses
P.O. Box 147
Deerfield, IL 60015

Lord and Burnham
2 Main Street
Irvington, NY 10533

McGregor Greenhouses
Box 36
Santa Cruz, CA 95063

National Greenhouse Company
P.O. Box 100
Pana, IL 62557

Sturdi-Built Manufacturing Company
11304 SW Boones Ferry Road
Portland, OR 97219

Texas Greenhouse Company
2717 St. Louis Avenue
Fort Worth, TX 76110

Turner Greenhouses
Box 1260
Goldsboro, NC 27530

Vegetable Factory, Inc.
100 Court Street
Copiague, NY 11726

SURFACES

American Olean Tile
2583 Cannon Avenue
Lansdale, PA 19446

The Asphalt Institute
Asphalt Institute Building
College Park, MD 20740

Binghamton Brick Company, Inc.
Box 1256
Binghamton, NY 13902

Bomanite Corporation
81 Encina Avenue
Palo Alto, CA 94301

Brick Institute of America
1750 Old Meadow Road
McLean, VA 22101

Formlite Products Inc.
2 Hughes Avenue
Rye, NY 10580

Kraftile Company
800 Kraftile Road
P.O. Box 2907
Fremont, CA 94536

National Concrete Masonry Association
P.O. Box 781
Herndon, VA 22070

Portland Cement Association
Old Orchard Road
Skokie, IL 60078

Wausau Tile
P.O. Box 1520
Wausau, WI 54401

Z-Brick
P.O. Box 628
Woodinville, WA 98072

LANDSCAPING, NURSERIES, AND GARDEN SUPPLY

Adams Nursery
Box 606, Route 20
Westfield, MA 01085

American Institute of Landscape Architects
501 East San Juan
Phoenix, AZ 85012

American Society of Landscape Architects
1733 Connecticut Avenue NW
Washington, DC 20009

Bachman's Inc.
6010 Lyndale Avenue South
Minneapolis, MN 55423

W. Atlee Burpee Company
300 Park Avenue
Warminster, PA 18974

Henry Field Seed and Nursery Company
407 Sycamore Street
Shenandoah, IA 51602

Greer Gardens
1280 Goodpasture Island Road
Eugene, OR 97401

Hastings
434 Marietta Street NW
Box 4274
Atlanta, GA 30302

Keil Brothers
220-15 Horace Harding Boulevard
Bayside, NY 11364

Lamb Nurseries
East 101M Sharp Avenue
Spokane, WA 99202

A.M. Leonard, Inc.
6665 Spiker Road
Piqua, OH 45356

Nuccio's Nurseries
3555 Chaney Trail
Box H
Altadena, CA 91001

Panfield Nurseries
322 Southdown Road
Huntington, NY 11743

Scarff's Nursery
Route 1
New Carlisle, OH 45344

Sprainbrook Nursery
448 Underhill Road
Scarsdale, NY 10583

William Tricker, Inc.
74 Allendale Road
Saddle River, NJ 07458

Waynesboro Nurseries
Route 664, Box 987
Waynesboro, VA 22980

Yerba Buena Nursery
19500 Skyline Boulevard
Woodside, CA 94062

GRILLS

Charmglow
Box 127
Bristol, WI 53104

PLAY EQUIPMENT

American Playground Device Company
P.O. Drawer 2599
Anderson, IN 46011

American Toy and Furniture
Company, Inc.
5933-T North Lincoln Avenue
Chicago, IL 60659

Big Toys
2601 South Hood Street
Tacoma, WA 98409

Child Life Play Specialties, Inc.
55 Whitney Street
Holliston, MA 01746

Children's Playgrounds, Inc.
P.O. Box 1563
Cambridge, MA 02238

Constructive Playthings
1040 East 85th Street
Kansas City, MO 64131

Davis-Grabowski, Inc.
6350 NE 4th Avenue
P.O. Box 381594
Miami, FL 33138

Game-Time Inc.
900 Anderson Road
Litchfield, MI 49252

Howell Playground Equipment Company
1718 East Fairchild Street
Danville, IL 61832

Outdoor Products Company
1759 Smith Avenue
P.O. Box 24527
San Jose, CA 95112

Patterson-Williams Manufacturing Company
651 Aldo Avenue
P.O. Box 4040
Santa Clara, CA 95050

Quadro America, Inc.
Room 662
200 Fifth Avenue
New York, NY

Quality Industries, Inc.
P.O. Box 1207
Hillsdale, MI 49242

Recreation Equipment Company
8th & John Streets
Anderson, IN 46011

The Stanley Works
P.O. Box 1800
New Britain, CT 06050

Trojan Playground Equipment
Manufacturing Company
11-T Second Avenue NE
St. Cloud, MN 56301

Vaughan and Associates, Inc.
2852 Walnut Hill Lane
Dallas, TX 75229

INDEX

▮ PHOTO CREDITS

Backyard Big Toys—p. 70

Bomanite Corp.—p. 86 (l)

John Dean—p. 29, 55

John Dominis/Wheeler—p. 91

Ken Druse—p. 16, 24-25, 40-41, 43 (l), 61, 78, 85

Susan Duane—p. 124

Dan Eifert—p. 43 (tr), 50, 69, 86 (r), 93, (Ruben de Saavedra, designer), 123 ([r] Linda Langsam, designer)

Phillip Ennis—p. 76-77

Derek Fell—p. 10-11, 13 (t), 20, 21, 27, 28, 30, 30-31, 36, 38, 45, 46, 46-47, 54, 58, 59 (l, r), 62-63, 65, 66, 68, 72, 74, 74-75, 79, 83, 94, 96, 97, 98, 100, 101, 102, 102-103, 108, 109, 110 (both), 112, 114, 120, 125 (both), 130, 131 (l), 132-133, 133, 134, 136 (l, r), 137

Felice Frankel—p. 136 (c)

Gaggenau—p. 57

Keith Glasgow—p. 13 (b), 15, 17, 22, 32, 32-33, 35 (t), 49 (r), 52, 99, 105, 113, 116, 131 (r)

Hammacher Schlemmer—p. 89

Heldor Industries, Inc.—p. 33, 84, 122

Jerry Howard/Positive Images—p. 8, 12 (t), 14-15, 24, 26, 31 (r), 33, 64, 67, 106, 107, 111, 114-115, 115, 129, 132

Robert Perron—p. 14 (t), 34, 48, 60, 75

Jonathan Pite—p. 103, 126-127

Quadro—p. 73

Shope, Reno, Wharton Associates, Greenwich, CT—p. 12 (b), 71

Steve Smith/Wheeler—p. 90

Tim Street-Porter—p. 18, 59 (c), 82, 128 (r), 135

Peter Tenzer/Wheeler—p. 92